TRIUMPHANT IN SUFFERING

Triumphant in Suffering

by MERLIN L. NEFF

Author of "Life Begins With God,"
"The Bible Pageant," "The Glory
of the Stars," "Power for Today"

PACIFIC PRESS PUBLISHING ASSOCIATION
Mountain View, California

Brookfield, Illinois   Omaha, Nebraska   Portland, Oregon

ACKNOWLEDGMENTS

Many of the Bible texts in this publication are from the *Revised Standard Version of the Bible*, copyrighted 1946 and 1952.

I wish to thank the following publishers for their co-operation in allowing me to quote from books bearing their imprint. Quotations are used with their special permission.

LEWIS, C. E., *The Problem of Pain*, The Macmillan Company, New York.

STEWART, JAMES E., *The Strong Name*, Charles Scribner's Sons, New York.

BOWIE, WALTER RUSSELL, *The Interpreter's Bible*, volume 1, Abingdon Press, Nashville.

SHIRES, HENRY H., and PIERSON PARKER, *The Interpreter's Bible*, volume 2, Abingdon Press, Nashville.

BUTTRICK, GEORGE A., *The Interpreter's Bible*, volume 7, Abingdon Press, Nashville.

GOSSIP, ARTHUR JOHN, *The Interpreter's Bible*, volume 8, Abingdon Press, Nashville.

SHORT, JOHN, *The Interpreter's Bible*, volume 10, Abingdon Press, Nashville.

REID, JAMES, *The Interpreter's Bible*, volume 10, Abingdon Press, Nashville.

CONTENTS

DEDICATED

To E. W. E., whose courage and fortitude
in the ordeal of suffering and sorrow has
been an inspiration in writing this volume.

PROLOGUE

To write about suffering, pain, and sorrow is one thing; to accept these unwelcome visitors when they come is quite another matter. I hesitate to write on this subject because I have not always triumphed in test. True, I have known weeks of illness and hours of intense pain, and at times it seems that from a horizontal position in bed I have gained a truer perspective of life, of my friends, and, most of all, of a loving God. But in some trials I have been bitter and rebellious; I have not accepted them patiently, and it has been difficult to pray, "Thy will be done." It is in these crises that I have devoted hours of study to find how it is possible to triumph over suffering.

No one enjoys suffering, and I am sorry to say that I believe it has often destroyed the best and noblest in human character. There are too many who feel as Somerset Maugham did when he expressed his views in these words: "I knew that suffering did not ennoble; it degraded. It made men selfish, mean, petty, and suspicious. It absorbed them in small things. It did not make them more than men; it made them less than men; and I wrote ferociously that we learn resignation not by our own suffering, but by the suffering of others."

This has been too often true, for man in his unconverted state is self-centered, not God-centered. And when there is faith in divine Providence, it is not always easy to "practice what we preach." Richard Sheppard, who endured torturing pain, wrote a friend: "I do not love suffering, so you must not worry about me in that way, and I dislike all that talk about how lovely it is to suffer. I think it is a rotten process, which has nothing whatever to do with God; at least, if God causes suffering and delights in it, I do not delight in believing in

Him. I know it may do me good—that is, if I take it decently, but I know it is as likely to embitter mankind as to convert him. There is a great deal of rot written, isn't there, about how beautiful it is for us to suffer?"

There is a great deal of truth in these cynical words. When men blame God for suffering, pain, and death, they turn against Him. Unless the thinking is straight and God's love is in the heart, suffering can turn a man from the way to heaven and drive him to destruction. It is of vital importance, then, that we face the truth and learn how to meet the universal problems that haunt men more today than in any previous age in history.

It is not the fleeting sorrow or the sharp pain of the moment that does the damage to the soul. A man who had suffered but little said, "I like pain, it brings me to God." Yet, later, when he had agonized for weeks and months, he grew disillusioned and cursed God. It is the suffering that goes on endlessly, the trial that seems purposeless that breaks the spirit. In the time of unceasing trial comes the greatest test. The nobility of character of men and women who have come through the dark valley of the shadow by trusting in a loving God who is at their side is the strongest proof that there is a better way to face tragedy. And the paramount proof is the example of Jesus Christ, who accepted the cup of sorrow and drank it to the dregs, for He was made "perfect through sufferings."

To our Example, our Saviour, we turn for lessons of faith. To Him we call: "Teach us how to be triumphant in suffering. Help us to find the divine answer for each trial and tribulation, that we may be conquerors through Thy name."

This is the fervent desire of the author for every reader and for himself.   THE AUTHOR.

Los Altos, California.

IS THERE AN ANSWER?

~∘‖∘~

How Sin and Suffering Came to Be

WHAT mysteries remain unsolved in this life! A sweet-faced little girl, innocent of wrong, lies in the hospital dying of a malignant tumor of the brain. Why should pain and death come to a child so young and eager for life?

A devoted minister of the gospel, driving through the night on a mission of mercy, sees the flash of headlights in his eyes, and then there is a crash. A drunk driver had swerved across the center line to hit the minister's car head-on. A godly man is killed instantly. Why did it happen to him when he was giving his life to the service of God?

Here is a Christian wife who has done all in her power to make a happy home for her husband and children. Now her happiness and security are shattered, as she becomes the victim of heartless desertion. Does God have an answer for this?

How are we to meet the bitter cup of pain and suffering? What is our reaction when heartaches and disappointments come? There are several ways human beings respond to suffering and sorrow. Some persons become bitter and resentful. They say, "If there is a God, why does He permit such things

to come? I don't believe He loves me." Dr. Harry Emerson
Fosdick tells of a man who said, "I don't know what I believe,
but I don't believe all this 'God is love' stuff. I've been in two
world wars, been unemployed eighteen months on end, seen
the missus die of cancer, and now I am waiting for atom bombs
to fall. All that stuff about Jesus is no help."

Others are stoical to calamity. They shrug their shoulders,
act calloused, and refuse to allow suffering to touch their
hearts. They consider life a mystery and simply say, "This,
too, will pass."

There are folk who pity themselves when faced with sorrow. With whimpering moans they say, "I must be a terrible
sinner, since all this trouble comes to me. I guess I was born
to suffer."

Then, again, there are a few men and women who do not
believe sorrow and pain exist. They attempt to deny the reality
of suffering, and say that there is no such thing as death.

Heartaches drive some persons to seek consolation in alcohol, frivolity, or riotous living, where they hope to drown their
sorrows. "Why not forget," they shout; "we only live a little
while, so why not have fun?"

Christianity Increases the Problem

We can see these reactions in the lives of those about us if
we only take time to look for them. Multitudes of Christians
have been puzzled as they attempted to reconcile faith in a
loving God with the bitter tragedies of life. One clergyman
says he has found it harder for Christians to accept and overcome sorrow than to gain the victory over doubt and sin. In
one sense this is true, for the person who does not accept the
gospel of Jesus Christ has no mystery to solve and no conflict
in his soul. The man without faith in Providence simply sub-

mits to what he calls "inevitable fate;" but the Christian declares that "God is love." The trusting soul must reconcile the dark and tragic experiences of life with his faith in the sovereignty of God. Thus, the Christian gospel of an all-loving heavenly Father thrusts the problem of suffering upon every believer, and it must be faced.

The mystery of suffering has been with mankind ever since the first family were upon the earth; however, the tensions and uncertainty of our day cause the questions to pile up with terrible urgency. Death comes suddenly, and millions of persons live on the razor's edge because of the ravages of war, famine, and disaster. The heavenly Father seems so far away from earth's welter and confusion that men lose their way in the darkness.

Since God is love and the basis of His government is the law of love, why are pain and sorrow and tragedy the lot of men? Only when we turn to the Bible do we find an answer that helps us to understand the problem. We shall never have the complete solution for the mystery of suffering, but we can fathom much of the divine plan for human beings.

To Goethe's statement, "If I were God, this world of sin and suffering would break my heart," I would answer, "That is what sin did to our Father's heart of love and to Jesus, our Saviour." Before this world was brought into existence, God faced the horrible menace of sin. Lucifer, the brilliant leader among the created beings of heaven, purposed in his heart to rebel against his Maker. The power of choice—a fearful instrument—had been given to the angelic host. They could love and obey God or they could follow their own selfish way. Lucifer decided to make self his god, for he exclaimed, "I will ascend into heaven, I will exalt my throne above the stars of God: I will sit also upon the mount of the congregation, in the sides of the north: I will ascend above the heights of the clouds; I will be like the Most High." Isaiah 14:13, 14.

Rebellion against God is sin. Thus when Lucifer and his cohorts made their fateful decision to revolt, they brought sin into a perfect universe. God permitted Lucifer, or Satan, to come to this earth. This rebel determined to tempt Adam and Eve, who were free moral agents, able to think and act as they chose. But the gift of freedom also carried with it the danger that man might forget his Creator and make the wrong choice.

God created this earth for perfect beings who would desire to follow His blueprint and obey His laws. Adam and Eve decided to turn the Garden of Eden into a place where they could do as they pleased. Their rebellious actions brought pain, sin, and death to the world.

The all-powerful God could have taken away the results of the first disobedient act of Adam and Eve; but then sin would have gone on and on unpunished, for the law would have been nullified. There would have been no consequences for wrongdoing, and no difference between good and evil. It would have robbed man of his power of choice since "sin is the transgression of the law," and where there is no law, there is no sin. The end result would, therefore, have been to make sin righteousness, for any code of law to be effective must have its penalties for disobedience.

As members of the human family we must accept the legacy of sin which is our inheritance; we cannot escape it. The apostle Paul describes man's plight in these words: "Therefore as sin came into the world through one man and death through sin, and so death spread to all men because all men sinned." Romans 5:12, R.S.V. The virus of evil spread throughout the world, and no one, except Jesus Christ, has been able to resist its deadly power, and that is why "the whole creation has been groaning in travail together until now." Romans 8:22, R.S.V.

What Causes Suffering?

This brings us face to face with the paramount issue: What are the causes of suffering? If we consider the chief reasons why pain and sorrow come, we shall know better how to relate ourselves to the problem.

1. *Suffering comes from the transgression of natural laws.* We live in a world where natural laws are in force. If they are disregarded or broken willfully, suffering is the result. A small child does not know about the law of gravitation, yet he toddles over a wall and falls to the hard pavement. He suffers pain as the penalty for breaking the law even though he did not know it existed. Should natural laws be suspended to save the innocent or ignorant from disaster? That is impossible, for everyone in the world would face chaos and destruction without these protective laws.

2. *Suffering may result from the wrong use of the power of choice.* Like Adam and Eve, modern men and women have brought disaster upon themselves by choosing the wrong course of action. Since we are free moral agents we can decide our course of action, but in the end we may find ourselves on the way of death. God could prohibit us from making foolish decisions, but by such intervention He would rob us of our freedom. Therefore, much of the pain and sorrow come upon us because the heavenly Father will not force us to do what is for our best good.

3. *Tragedies may result from man's greedy exploitation of nature.* Sometimes human beings blame God for the disasters in nature, such as floods and pestilences. While they are beyond

the control of the individuals who suffer, yet some of these catastrophes are the result of the selfish actions of men. A flood may sweep away a thousand homes and cause the death of five hundred persons; but the real reason for the disaster is man's ruthless, wasteful destruction of the forests which once held back the flood waters. We cannot squander the natural resources given us by the Creator without paying the penalty.

4. *Some tragedy and disaster is brought about by satanic power operating on the forces of nature.* Certain destructive forces, such as earthquakes and tornadoes, are beyond man to influence or control; yet they are not acts of a loving Father. When man lost his earthly dominion, Satan became "the prince of the power of the air." Ephesians 2:2. Unless restrained by God, this fearful enemy can wreak havoc and death by making nature a destroyer. "In accidents and calamities by sea and by land, in great conflagrations, in fierce tornadoes and terrific hailstorms, in tempests, floods, cyclones, tidal waves, and earthquakes, in every place and in a thousand forms, Satan is exercising his power. He sweeps away the ripening harvest, and famine and distress follow."—*The Great Controversy,* pages 589, 590.

5. *Pain and death may result from the careless mistakes of human beings.* Since we live in an imperfect world where men make mistakes or shirk their responsibility, accidents are bound to occur. An airplane crashes, snuffing out sixty lives. If the truth were known, the airliner came to grief because a mechanic was careless in his work, the inspector had not checked the equipment thoroughly, or the pilot was weary and misjudged his position. The God who loves men does not always see fit to perform a miracle to save the innocent from human error or poor judgment.

6. *Heartaches and bloodshed are caused by political and*

economic dictators. Suffering and sorrow have been the fate of millions of innocent souls because of oppressors. Tyrants have risen in power and sent armies marching to their death. God does not instigate wars; He is a loving Father who knows only love and peace. War is basically the result of man's rebellion against the divine will; and the dead and wounded, the displaced persons and innocent children, suffer because of man's inhumanity to man, not because God wants the ordeal of blood and tears.

The Christian can be certain that the basic cause of all sorrow and suffering is sin—not God. "Sickness, suffering, and death are work of an antagonistic power. Satan is the destroyer; God is the restorer."—*The Ministry of Healing,* page 113.

A Call to the Prodigal

God may permit trial and tragedy to test His children, but "He does not willingly afflict or grieve the sons of men." Lamentations 3:33, R.S.V. Suffering and loss may be the only way that a loving God can penetrate the calloused shell of the person who rests smugly in his carnal pleasures, his foolish thinking, and his sins. Rich and increased in material blessings, he finds no need of God until pain and sorrow strike. C. S. Lewis well says: "God whispers to us in our pleasures, speaks in our conscience, but shouts in our pain: it is His megaphone to rouse a deaf world."—*The Problem of Pain,* page 81.

To the Christian, then, suffering is not so much a mystery to be solved as a challenge to be met. We have the assurance that we are not alone in the darkness, for God is by our side. The sweet comfort of the twenty-third psalm centers in the knowledge that the Eternal One is with us. "Yea, though I walk through the valley of the shadow of death, I will fear no evil: for Thou art with me."

In the final chapter of *A Tale of Two Cities* Charles Dickens gives a moving description of two prisoners in Paris riding in a cart to the guillotine. One is a brave man who had once lost his way but had found it again, and who is now dying for a friend. Beside the man is another prisoner—a young girl. She saw the gentleness and courage of this man at the prison, and as she faces death, she asks to ride in the cart with him. "If I may ride with you," says the frightened girl, "will you let me hold your hand? . . . I am little and weak, and it will give me more courage."

So the two prisoners ride in the cart to the place of execution. As the girl gets out of the cart, she looks into the face of the friend and says, "I think you were sent to me by heaven."

In a far closer way Jesus Christ is with us in every hour of trial and sorrow. When Israel suffered at the hand of enemies, these words of comfort were spoken: "In all their affliction He was afflicted, and the angel of His presence saved them: in His love and in His pity He redeemed them; and He bare them, and carried them all the days of old." Isaiah 63:9.

If at each day's beginning we will place our hand in the hand of Jesus, the ever-old, ever-new miracle will take place again, and our broken hearts and tear-dimmed eyes will find comfort as we look up with hope into the face of our loving heavenly Father who does all things well.

MEN WHO ENDURED SUFFERING

~~2~~

Abraham, Jacob, Moses, and Paul

IT IS one thing to theorize as to how suffering should be accepted; it is quite another matter to experience it. I have known ministers who preached submission to God's will for years, but when tragedy came they rebelled against it in a fury of bitterness. The problem of pain never seems urgent or imperative until it comes into our own life. I remember a man who visited me in the hospital after I had gone through months of suffering. He had never been sick in his life, but he glibly said, "I sympathize with you in your illness." I also remember when a relative sat beside me and with deep emotion said, "You have suffered a great deal. I know, for I've been through the same attacks again and again."

Talking about sorrow and suffering from a distance is easy, but looking at pain from the inside through tears makes a person humble and silent. It is well, therefore, to look at the lives of men of the Bible who are examples of faith and patience in trial and suffering. We are admonished by the apostle

(9)

James to consider the prophets as "an example of suffering affliction, and of patience." James 5:10.

To see a fellow traveler on life's highway endure the same tests and temptations that we experience and come through triumphantly is a source of spiritual strength. That is why the experiments in the laboratory of life recorded in Holy Writ are so precious to the trusting Christian.

"These examples of human steadfastness, in the might of divine power, are a witness to the world of the faithfulness of God's promises—of His abiding presence and sustaining grace. As the world looks upon these humble men, it cannot discern their moral value with God. It is a work of faith to calmly repose in God in the darkest hour—however severely tried and tempest-tossed, to feel that our Father is at the helm."—*Testimonies,* vol. 4, p. 525.

In the lives of the four characters to be considered in this chapter, we find four types of sorrow and suffering. Abraham's greatest ordeal was a trial of faith. Was he willing to obey God by offering his son as a human sacrifice? The suffering and anxiety of Jacob was largely the result of sin in his own life. He reaped the harvest of his own sowing, yet from the bitter experience he came forth a new man. Moses accepted the cup of humiliation, personal loss, and tribulation, because he loved his people. He was willing to give up honor and wealth to obey God's call. Finally, Paul is a study of a valiant man who knew physical and mental agony. He was persecuted because he preached the gospel; yet in the midst of fiery trials he rejoiced to be worthy to suffer for Christ.

Abraham, a Man of Faith

Faith does not spring full-blown in the life of a great man; it is developed through years of testing. Such was the experience of Abraham, the pioneer, who left his Chaldean homeland, his friends, and most of his relatives for a strange country whose distance to him could be compared only with a journey halfway around the world today. God's purpose gripped the adventurer as he set out, "not knowing where he was to go." This patriarch had many detours on his way. He stopped first in Haran, where he lived long enough to feel at home and where he was tempted to remain in a comfortable existence. He could have reasoned that this was all that God could expect of him. Why go farther? But Abraham was made of stronger stuff; he was not disobedient to the divine call. He pushed on and arrived in Canaan, where "by faith he sojourned in the land of promise, as in a foreign land, living in tents." Hebrews 11:9, R.S.V.

A detour into Egypt, the lack of co-operation on the part of his nephew Lot, and the necessity of rescuing him from kidnapers, were troublesome episodes in Abraham's development. Poor Lot was weak spiritually. He "lifted up his eyes" toward Sodom, and he "pitched his tent toward Sodom," then he "dwelt in Sodom." Finally, when escape from the wicked city was offered to the vacillating man and his family, "he lingered" in Sodom. Yet through all his trials, and in spite of family burdens, Abraham did not waver, for he was bound to God by cords of faith.

However, the most severe ordeal came in the sunset years of Abraham and Sarah's life, after they had been given Isaac, through whom God promised to develop the chosen nation. Abraham must have staggered when he received the divine command: "Take now thy son, thine only son Isaac, whom thou lovest, and get thee into the land of Moriah; and offer him there for a burnt offering." Genesis 22:2.

Human sacrifices to pagan deities were a common practice

among the Canaanite tribes; but the true God had never asked His children to take human life. Abraham must have wondered at times if he should not be willing to do as much as the pagans did, if his God commanded.

We must never minimize the suffering and sorrow that this man of faith endured. It was, no doubt, the greatest anyone had experienced up to that time. "The trial was far more severe than that which had been brought upon Adam. Compliance with the prohibition laid upon our first parents involved no suffering; but the command to Abraham demanded the most agonizing sacrifice. All heaven beheld with wonder and admiration Abraham's unfaltering obedience. All heaven applauded his fidelity."—*Patriarchs and Prophets,* page 155.

The test ended in victory! God could say to His servant, "Now I know that thou fearest God, seeing thou hast not withheld thy son, thine only son from Me." Genesis 22:12. What do we attempt to hold back as too precious to place on the altar of sacrifice? Only a boundless devotion, an unlimited commitment, will stand the test. Like Abraham, each of us is faced with a supreme moment when we must decide if we will pay the price to follow God all the way. May it be said of us, as it was of this patriarch of old, "By faith Abraham . . . obeyed."

Suffering for His Sins

Although man brings sorrow and suffering upon himself because of his sins, yet if he is truly repentant he can, like Jacob, gain a blessed victory. The early pages of Jacob's life present him as a rogue and a rascal. It all began in a home where parental love was divided, where jealousy and dissension reigned. As Robertson points out, "Rebekah loved her son more than truth, i.e., more than God. . . . Abraham was ready to sacrifice his son to duty. Rebekah sacrificed truth and duty to her son."—*Sermons on Bible Subjects,* pages 27, 28.

By seeking the birthright, Jacob revealed his longing for spiritual values and his need for a close relationship to God; but he lacked faith. Therefore he endeavored to work out his salvation in his own way, and this brought him sorrow, suffering, and very nearly cost him his life.

As a refugee in Haran, Jacob received some of the treatment he had given to others—he was deceived and cheated. The years passed and Jacob realized it was time for him to take his large family back to Canaan if he would keep them in the faith of the true God. But the supplanter must face his brother, and what would be the outcome of this meeting?

"Jacob was greatly afraid and distressed" when he found that Esau was coming to meet him with four hundred men. The angels of God stood by Jacob on the way, and they gave him renewed courage, even as they had done years before at Bethel. He called the place Mahanaim, which means: "This is God's army!" Genesis 32:2, R.S.V. But the man had not completed his course in humility; he must be humbled and chastened by suffering and by a night of wrestling at the brook Jabbok.

Through the dark hours Jacob struggled with his supposed adversary. "While he was thus battling for his life, the sense of his guilt pressed upon his soul; his sins rose up before him, to shut him out from God. But in his terrible extremity he remembered God's promises, and his whole heart went out in entreaty for His mercy."—*Patriarchs and Prophets,* page 197.

Haunted by uncertainty and burdened by our sins, how many of us wrestle blindly as did Jacob! We could have comfort and help in the instant of our need; but we fight on, hoping to gain the victory in our own strength. Finally, in our helplessness we cry out for divine strength and blessing; and, lo, God has been at our side all the time! Jacob wrestled from darkness to sunrise, for we read that "the sun rose upon him as he passed Penuel."

Victory came to Jacob as he held on to God through pain and tears. "Caught in the grip of judgment, his prevailing desire was not for escape. He would hold on until something decisive happened. . . . The shallow man may ignore his sins; the cowardly man may try to evade their consequences; but Jacob now was neither one."—*The Interpreter's Bible,* vol. 1, p. 724. Now Jacob was "a prince of God," for he had found the true source of power—a humble and contrite heart obedient to God.

Moses, Patient in Trial

The greatest men in history are those who have cast their lot with the oppressed and downtrodden. Again, some of the best work has been done by those who felt unfitted for the task. Moses is classified with both of these groups. He chose "rather to share ill treatment with the people of God than to enjoy the fleeting pleasures of sin" in the idolatrous land of Egypt. Hebrews 11:25, R.S.V. He joined his people in their suffering and slavery, for "he considered abuse suffered for the Christ greater wealth than the treasures of Egypt, for he looked to the reward." Verse 26, R.S.V.

Here was the secret of the man's power: By faith Moses looked beyond the trials and tribulations of the moment to the final reward. "He looked beyond the gorgeous palace, beyond a monarch's crown, to the high honors that will be bestowed on the saints of the Most High in a kingdom untainted by sin. He saw by faith an imperishable crown that the King of heaven would place on the brow of the overcomer. This faith led him to turn away from the lordly ones of earth, and join the humble, poor, despised nation that had chosen to obey God rather than to serve sin."—*Patriarchs and Prophets,* page 246.

"Why do you say Moses suffered ill treatment with the people of God?" someone may ask. "He was the leader of the nation. Surely he had power and honor in his position." When Moses accepted the divine call to lead Israel from Egypt he took upon himself a lonely, thankless task in which he would be misunderstood by the multitude. He was an outcast from all his Egyptian friends; his own brother and sister arose against him on occasion, and the thousands of Israelites rebelled against his leadership and threatened to kill him.

Yet, when the way became too rough and rebellion was in the camp, Moses pleaded with God for strength and courage. When the nation sank into idolatry and God was ready to destroy the people for their sin, Moses stood firm in intercession for them. He courageously asked that his name be blotted out of the book of life if God could not save the nation. In other words, Moses loved his people so completely that he was willing to face annihilation with them if they could not be forgiven.

Yet this Gibraltar of a man failed in a minor crisis! At Meribah the people shouted for water, and God commanded Moses and Aaron to "tell the rock before their eyes to yield its water." Numbers 20:8, R.S.V. But Moses called the thirsty crowd "rebels" and struck the rock twice. God did not fail to supply the people with water, even though Moses had disobeyed. The rock, a symbol of Christ, had once been smitten; it should not have been struck again. But in this moment Moses lacked faith, and he "lost sight of his Almighty Helper. . . . The man who might have stood pure, firm, and unselfish to the close of his work, had been overcome at last."—*Patriarchs and Prophets,* page 418.

Now Moses suffered before the entire nation. Every Israelite knew their leader had sinned and that he must receive humiliating punishment. He had given his life for the nation, and he longed to lead them triumphantly into the Promised Land; but it was not to be. Listen to his farewell speech to the throng standing before him: "I am a hundred and twenty years old this day; I am no longer able to go out and come in. The Lord has said to me, 'You shall not go over this Jordan.'" Deuteronomy 31:2, R.S.V.

In seeming defeat, the mighty warrior for God was not bowed or broken. He introduced Joshua as the new leader and then gave this ringing testimony: "Be strong and of good courage, . . . for it is the Lord your God who goes with you; He will not fail you or forsake you." Verse 6, R.S.V.

Suffering, trial, and disappointment faded from the mind of Moses. He had confessed his sin, received forgiveness, and he was now ready for a mountaintop experience with his God. "From the human point of view, which loves happy endings, the story should have been rounded out with Moses leading his people over the Jordan. . . . If God chooses to close a door, no lasting disappointments can beset the life which is fully committed to Him."—*The Interpreter's Bible,* vol. 2, p. 535.

Moses needed no tomb or monument to mark his resting place, for soon after his death he was raised to life and ascended with his Deliverer to the glories of heaven.

Paul, a Triumphant Sufferer

If any Bible character was truly qualified to write on the subject of suffering, it was Paul, who loved the title "an apostle of Jesus Christ." He endured physical infirmity, which he called his "thorn in the flesh;" and although he prayed earnestly that it be taken away, it was not God's will to remove it. For years Paul experienced bitter persecution—physical and mental —in order to preach the gospel of his Lord. In addition to this he had heartbreaking disappointments because of strife among the church members and the apostasy of some believers. Paul declared that suffering was a part of the Christian's life, and he affirmed that where sin and suffering abounded, the grace and comfort of God must much more abound.

What physical ailment Paul suffered, we are not informed. He "suggests that it was painful, crippling his enjoyment of life, and frustrating his full efficiency. It was also humiliating, for it awoke in others the pity which is sometimes mingled with contempt."—*The Interpreter's Bible,* vol. 10, p. 407. The apostle says it was given "to harass me, to keep me from being too elated. Three times I besought the Lord about this, that it should leave me; but He said to me, 'My grace is sufficient for you, for My power is made perfect in weakness.' " 2 Corinthians 12:7-9, R.S.V.

God answered Paul's prayer with "No." A true Christian will be content with this answer, for he is submissive to God's will. In the case of the apostle, God assured him that there was ample strength and grace from heaven to meet his need. So Paul could say, "I will all the more gladly boast of my weaknesses, that the power of Christ may rest upon me." Verse 9, R.S.V.

Here is a statement of what suffering can do to the spiritually minded man. The weakness, the pain, the physical defect, can be transformed into a blessing! Suffering oftentimes breaks down our self-sufficiency and makes us willing to follow the Holy Spirit's leading. Tragedy can take boasting from our lives and cause us to glory in the cross of Calvary. Writing of John Bunyan's trials, W. Hale White declares, "The Creator gets the appointed task out of His servants in many ways. It is sufficient to give some of them love, sunrises and sunsets, and primrose woods in spring: others have to be scourged with bloody whips . . . before they do what God has determined for them."—*John Bunyan,* pages 25, 26.

Paul was reminded again and again that he was "a frail vessel of earth." 2 Corinthians 4:7, Moffatt. Yet he was made of the toughest metal, for he endured the ordeal of beating with rods, stoning, shipwreck, imprisonment in dungeons, as well as hunger, cold, and nakedness.

Near the beginning of his ministry, Paul, accompanied by Silas, was illegally beaten, thrown in prison, and fastened in stocks. Yet the two missionaries prayed and sang while they suffered in the Philippian jail. "From the inner prison, voices broke the silence of midnight with songs of joy and praise to God. These disciples were cheered by a deep and earnest love for the cause of their Redeemer, for which they suffered."— *Testimonies,* vol. 3, p. 406.

In his second letter to the church at Corinth, Paul gives a series of four dramatic contrasts in his experience. He says, "We are afflicted in every way, but not crushed; perplexed, but not driven to despair; persecuted, but not forsaken; struck down, but not destroyed." 2 Corinthians 4:8, 9, R.S.V.

When we realize that these experiences came to Paul *because* he was following Jesus Christ and preaching His gospel, we catch a deeper insight into the apostle's dauntless spirit. No wonder John Buchan has said: "I reckon fortitude's the biggest thing a man can have—just to go on enduring when there's no . . . heart left in you. . . . The head man at the job was the apostle Paul."—*Mr. Standfast,* page 177.

How much it means, then, for Paul to write of the "God of all comfort, who comforts us in all our affliction." 2 Corinthians 1:3, 4, R.S.V. Comfort is not a sedative to deaden the pain; it is a strengthener. The word comes from the same root as "fortify." God was with Paul, comforting, or building him up, in all his afflictions. The comfort from our heavenly Father comes through facing the truth about ourselves and accepting the divine will for our life. Like the man of Tarsus, we must come to the place where we will say, "I can do all things"—suffer, face perplexities, come to the end of all my resources, lose loved ones, and meet death—"in Him who strengthens me."

Most amazing of all, Paul could declare truthfully that "we rejoice in our sufferings, knowing that suffering produces endurance, and endurance produces characer, and character produces hope, and hope does not disappoint us, because God's love has been poured into our hearts through the Holy Spirit which has been given to us." Romans 5:3-5, R.S.V. The apostle saw that the fire of trial and affliction burned out the dross and, with the help of the Holy Spirit, developed character that would be fit for heaven.

Finally, Paul, the dynamic man of action, was in prison—first in Jerusalem, then in Caesarea, and finally at Rome. These must have been tedious months and years for the apostle who had known so much activity. During this time some of his fellow workers were called away or gave up the faith. When trial and imprisonment came, Paul watched for God's plan to turn barriers into blessings for the furtherance of the gospel.

The lesson was so indelibly written in Paul's life that he longed to share Christ's sufferings. Philippians 3:10. Like a trumpet peal his message sounded to Timothy: "The time of my departure has come. I have fought the good fight, I have finished the race, I have kept the faith." 2 Timothy 4:6, 7, R.S.V. Beyond all suffering and tragedy, Paul saw Jesus at the end of the road with the crown of glory. The doughty apostle had lived a committed life, and for him the reward was sure!

DAVID'S VICTORY OVER SORROW

∼3∼

A Man Who Faced Many Crises

T O FEEL deeply one must have strong emotions and keen senses. Such a person knows the height of gladness and feels the pangs of sorrow more intensely than does the average man in the street. David, the son of Jesse, was extremely sensitive to beauty in nature, to the Creator's handiwork and power, and to love. He could be described as a man with a poetic soul who yearned for the presence of God in his life.

While caring for his father's sheep on the hills of Bethlehem, the young man may have composed and sung many spiritual psalms, such as this:

> "The heavens are telling the glory of God;
>   and the firmament proclaims His handiwork.
> Day to day pours forth speech,
>   and night to night declares knowledge.
> There is no speech, nor are there words;
>   their voice is not heard;
> yet their voice goes out through all the earth,
>   and their words to the end of the world."
>   Psalm 19:1-4, R.S.V.

Or again he may have blended his voice with the music of his harp to sing:

> "As a hart longs for flowing streams,
> so longs my soul for Thee, O God.
> My soul thirsts for God, for the living God.
> When shall I come and behold the face of God?
> My tears have been my food day and night,
> while men say to me continually,
>   'Where is your God?' "
>
> Psalm 42:1-3, R.S.V.

Because he was of a sensitive nature, David suffered intensely when he sinned or when sorrow and loss bowed his spirit. "The love that moved him, the sorrows that beset him, the triumphs that attended him, were all themes for his active thought. . . . While he was absorbed in deep meditation, and harassed by thoughts of anxiety, he turned to his harp, and called forth strains that elevated his mind to the Author of every good, and the dark clouds that seemed to shadow the horizon of the future were dispelled."—*Patriarchs and Prophets,* pages 642-644.

Called to Be King

We first see David as a youth hurrying in from the meadow at the command of his father. The bronzed shepherd boy, who lived much in the outdoors, was met by the prophet Samuel; and before Jesse's seven other sons the youngest member of the family was anointed king of Israel. The character of David at this period of his life is revealed in the testimony of one of Saul's servants. "Behold, I have seen a son of Jesse the Bethlehemite," he declared, "who is skillful in playing, a man of valor, a man of war, prudent in speech, and a man of good presence; and the Lord is with him." 1 Samuel 16:18, R.S.V.

Indomitable faith in the Lord was shown by David when he stood before giant Goliath and said, "You come to me with a sword and with a spear and with a javelin; but I come to you in the name of the Lord of hosts, the God of the armies of Israel, whom you have defied." 1 Samuel 17:45, R.S.V. With exultant courage young David added, "The battle is the Lord's and He will give you into our hand." Verse 47.

The first period of suffering in the life of David was the unjust and undeserved persecution by King Saul. The acknowledged leader of God's people had departed from God's way, and at this time he was actually an impostor. It must have almost shaken David's faith to receive such cruel treatment from the reigning monarch, especially after the youth had been told by the prophet that he was the true king! After all, a child of God suffers no more baffling discouragement than to find cunning, sinister evil wrought against him by a professed leader in God's cause. When the wrath of the half-insane king fell upon David, the youth became a fugitive, fleeing day and night for his life, for "Saul became David's enemy continually." 1 Samuel 18:29. The young man who had a short time before been set apart as God's choice to rule Israel was now an outcast, forced to desert his wife and friends, and to wander in deserts and hide in caves—even seeking refuge among the despised Philistines.

Recounting these years of sorrow and suffering, David wrote:

> "I call upon the Lord, who is worthy to be praised,
>   and I am saved from my enemies.
> The cords of death encompassed me,
>   the torrents of perdition assailed me;
> the cords of Sheol entangled me,
>   the snares of death confronted me."
>   Psalm 18:3-6, R.S.V.

The psalmist realized that suffering could change character and alter one's attitude toward life. The word "character" comes from Greek derivation meaning *to cut out, to carve or engrave* as with a graving tool. Affliction is the sharp instrument with which much of the divine carving is accomplished. If we allow the knife to cut away defects and shape us, we shall eventually be fashioned according to the pattern of the Master.

During the months and years that Saul persecuted David it was difficult for the sufferer to see the hand of God in his stormy experiences. Yet we are told that "it was the providence of God that had connected David with Saul. . . . The vicissitudes and hardships which befell him, through the enmity of Saul, would lead him to feel his dependence upon God, and to put his whole trust in Him. . . . In all these things, God was working out His gracious purposes, both for David and for the people of Israel."—*Patriarchs and Prophets,* page 649.

David Ascends the Throne

After the death of Saul, David was crowned king of Israel, and during his reign he established his court at Jerusalem. For many years he was a faithful ruler, bringing the golden ark to the new capital city and setting his people an example in devotion and worship of the true God. The nation prospered in an era of peace, and when enemies rose up—as did the Philistines and Moabites—David's armies subdued them in glorious victories.

Finally, a group of enemy nations swept down from the north and east to attack Israel. Joab, the general of David's army, possessed the courage of his king, for he called upon his men to put their trust in God. "Be of good courage," he said, "and let us play the man for our people, and for the cities of our God; and may the Lord do what seems good to Him."

1 Chronicles 19:13, R.S.V. While the armies were marching, David was humbly praying for the salvation of his people. "The dangers which had threatened the nation with utter destruction, proved, through the providence of God, to be the very means by which it rose to unprecedented greatness."—*Patriarchs and Prophets,* page 715. Later the king sang praises to God for victories won:

> "The Lord lives; and blessed be my Rock,
>   and exalted be the God of my salvation,
>   the God who gave me vengeance
>   and subdued peoples under me;
>   who delivered me from my enemies;
>   yea, Thou didst exalt me above my adversaries;
>   Thou didst deliver me from men of violence."
>   Psalm 18:46-48, R.S.V.

However, it was in the time of his greatest prosperity and martial triumph that David was in the greatest danger. It is not easy to carry the brimming cup of success with Christian humility. In his self-sufficiency, the king forgot God and yielded to subtle temptations of the flesh. Adultery was written against David's name, and when, as the result of his illicit passion for Bath-sheba, he was trapped, the king attempted to cover one transgression with still another—the murder of Uriah. David should have remembered the wise words of Moses that echoed down the centuries: "Be sure your sin will find you out." He should have realized that he could not hide his evil course from the eyes of God. For about a year he seemed to be secure in his wickedness, although his conscience gnawed within him. Later he described his agony in these words:

> "When I declared not my sin, my body wasted away
>   through my groaning all day long.

> For day and night Thy hand was heavy upon me; *
> my strength was dried up as by the heat of summer."
>
> Psalm 32:3, 4, R.S.V.

Then into the court of the king came the prophet Nathan with a divine accusation. He described the cancer of sin, and then said to David, "Thou art the man." Judgments were to fall in succeeding years upon the king's head, for the prophecy declared that "the sword shall never depart from thine house." The news of David's sins was broadcast throughout the nation, and the people recognized that he should rightfully receive the punishment of death; yet no man dared lift his hand against the ruler.

Staggered by the enormity of his evil deeds and broken in spirit, David confessed his transgressions. "I have sinned against the Lord," he whispered with bowed head. In such an hour Satan must have gloated, for here was the one person in all Israel he desired most to bring to ruin. Was he not the anointed king that had been chosen by the Lord? Was he not the spiritual leader of his people? Behold him now, crushed, defeated, and seemingly lost!

But in the agony of his suffering, David found the divine healing balm of forgiveness. Nathan said to the king, "The Lord also has put away your sin; you shall not die. Nevertheless, because by this deed you have utterly scorned the Lord, the child that is born to you shall die." 2 Samuel 12:13, 14, R.S.V.

We will never fully understand why the innocent must sometimes suffer for the sins of others; yet a gleam of light breaks through the clouds and we faintly comprehend. In this instance we see that God used the loss of the innocent baby to bring David to full repentance. In this experience "the king was given opportunity for repentance; while to him the suffering and death of the child, as a part of his punishment, was far more bitter than his own death could have been."—*Patriarchs and Prophets,* page 722. When our path goes through some of the darkest chasms of suffering it would be far sweeter to lie down and rest in death than to fight on through blood and tears. It is sometimes far greater punishment to live and endure the ignominy and pain than to be able to by-pass it by the sleep of death.

When the message reached David that his little son was dead, the king bowed his head and accepted the decree of the Almighty. We can better understand David's spiritual struggle, his suffering, and his final victory over sin when we read these verses from the fifty-first psalm:

"Have mercy on me, O God, according to Thy steadfast love;
    according to Thy abundant mercy blot out my transgressions.
Wash me thoroughly from my iniquity,
    and cleanse me from my sin!"
                                Verses 1, 2, R.S.V.

In these four lines of poetry David uses three words to describe his sin. *Pesha,* "transgression," is the act of setting one's self defiantly against God's will and rebelling against His eternal law. *Awon,* "iniquity," best describes a "warped" or "crooked" course. And *hatah,* "sin," means "to miss the mark." Therefore the psalmist recognizes that sin is a rebellion against God that leads to a crooked course of action, a course that takes one far from the mark God has set before us. David longed for his sins to be blotted out so that he might stand clean and pure before his Maker. This is the keynote of his soul-searching petition, as found in verses 10 to 12:

"Create in me a clean heart, O God,
    and put a new and right spirit within me.
Cast me not away from Thy presence,
    and take not Thy Holy Spirit from me.

Restore to me the joy of Thy salvation,
and uphold me with a willing spirit."

How wonderful it is to know that sins are blotted out and
to feel peace come to the troubled conscience! This assurance
of pardon, forgiveness, and a return to sonship in the Father's
house has been made certain for every sinner through the
death of Jesus Christ. Our Saviour is a mighty Redeemer, and
through Him we can know the joy of freedom from all sin!

Suffering Because of Weakness

There is no greater tragedy than for a father, who dearly
loves his son, to be so indulgent of the youth that he winks at
his faults and fails in discipline. Then the day comes when an
avalanche of sorrow crashes down on the father's head because
of the crimes of the wayward boy—crimes for which the father
is actually responsible. This was the additional suffering that
David had to endure.

The king of Israel failed to punish his first-born son Amnon
for his shameful crime. No doubt David refused to act because
he was haunted by the weakness in his own character. When
two years were allowed to pass without the indulgent son's
being punished, Absalom stepped in and murdered his brother.

The real reason for the tragedy in the family is found in
these words: "David had neglected the duty of punishing the
crime of Amnon, and because of the unfaithfulness of the king
and father, and the impenitence of the son, the Lord permitted
events to take their natural course, and did not restrain Absalom. When parents or rulers neglect the duty of punishing
iniquity, God Himself will take the case in hand. His restrain-
ing power will be in a measure removed from the agencies of
evil, so that a train of circumstances will arise which will
punish sin with sin."—*Patriarchs and Prophets,* page 728.

Many a brokenhearted father or mother has pleaded with God to turn a prodigal son back to the path of right, to save the child from sin, when if the truth were known, the youth had been petted, pampered, and allowed to go in a rebellious course during the years of childhood. In later life he reaps the harvest of his and his parent's sowing. God cannot step in and force the sanctity of the human will, even to save a rebellious child from his crimes that will disgrace the family and bring unmeasured suffering to the parents.

After his failure with Amnon, David also blundered in his dealings with Absalom. First he alienated him for his crime, and later he allowed him to return to Jerusalem but refused to make peace with him. Absalom courted the favor of the citizenry until he "stole the hearts of the men of Israel." Soon there was open rebellion and revolt, and David fled from Jerusalem for fear of being assassinated.

We see the full cup of sorrow that the king must drink as he once more became a pitiful fugitive. "In humility and sorrow, David passed out of the gate of Jerusalem,—driven from his throne, from his palace, from the ark of God, by the insurrection of his cherished son. The people followed in long, sad procession, like a funeral train."—*Patriarchs and Prophets,* page 731.

Wise, indeed, is the person who sees the meaning of sorrow and profits by it. David "saw in his own sin the cause of his trouble," and again he turned to God for mercy and pardon. The Lord permitted "David to pass under the rod, but He did not destroy him; the furnace is to purify, but not to consume." —*Ibid.,* p. 738. Our heavenly Father seeks to purify the character, not to consume the life of His beloved child.

Forgiveness is not all that the Christian needs. Each follower of the Master must also have the sustaining love of God, the upholding power of the everlasting arms. David's sins were blotted out, but the scars—the remorse, the heartaches—remained. The prophet had told him, "The sword shall never depart from thine house." His little son died, and his other sons brought him disgrace. In his sunset years, when men long for peace and calm, David was crushed by Absalom's rebellion and death. Yet through the dark hours—and there were many in David's life—he learned to wait for the deliverance that came from heaven. He exclaimed:

> "My soul waits for the Lord
> more than watchmen for the morning."
> Psalm 130:6, R.S.V.

Truly "the psalms of David pass through the whole range of experience, from the depths of conscious guilt and self-condemnation to the loftiest faith and the most exalted communing with God."—*Patriarchs and Prophets,* page 754. That is why every Christian finds comfort and strength there, for in them he learns that God is his Comforter and Shepherd, his Refuge and Rock of salvation.

Shadows may have a valuable place in life, as explained by Thomas R. Henry in writing about the cold continent of Antarctica. He says, "In white darkness there are no shadows; these are seen only when the sun is high in a cloudless sky. As a result Antarctica most of the time is a shadowless land. On a cloudy day the illumination of the landscape is so diffuse that there is no perspective by which one can estimate the contours, size, or distance of white objects. The feet cannot find the snow underfoot. One staggers and stumbles like a drunken man. Walking becomes extremely difficult and tiresome. Sledge and tractor drivers cannot move for days at a time until shadows reappear by which they can detect the parallel ridges which indicate the presence of crevasses. Otherwise they might well stumble blindfolded into an area crisscrossed with thousand-foot-deep rifts in the ice which are the death traps of polar explorers.

"Elsewhere, perhaps, shadows do not play an important part in life. But in the infinity of whiteness, black images on the snow provide a pattern by which the human mind can function. Without them the difficulties of finding one's way are enormously multiplied. They may mean the difference between reason and utter confusion—in extreme cases between life and death. Where all reality is white it vanishes in whiteness, and the world is left empty of substance."—*The White Continent,* pages 39, 40.

The shadows helped David find the true persepective in life as he turned to God with all his heart. If the Eternal One allows us to pass through deep waters, may we, like the psalmist, be able to say:

> "Search me, O God, and know my heart!
> Try me and know my thoughts!
> And see if there be any wicked way in me,
> and lead me in the way everlasting!"
> Psalm 139:23, 24, R.S.V.

"I SHALL COME FORTH
AS GOLD"

⚜4⚜

A Saint Suffers for His Faith

SOONER or later everybody needs a faith or philosophy of
life big enough and strong enough to stand up to disaster,"
said Leslie D. Weatherhead. "Blessed is he who has his
anchor secure before the storm breaks. When what we call
disaster breaks upon us, we are too stunned to be able to ar-
range our ideas, too bewildered to begin to erect our faith."

Job came to terms with God before he faced the white-hot
flames of suffering, and he knew he could depend on his
Redeemer. Yet the mystery of suffering Job faced was so
baffling, that although the Lord said this man was "perfect
and upright, and one that feared God, and eschewed evil" (Job
1:1), yet when sorrow cascaded over the poor man, he cursed
the day he was born and wished he were dead.

There is a significant warning in the book of Job—a warning against twisted thinking that believes doing right guaran-
tees prosperity and that wickedness always reaps its harvest of
tears in this life. It has always been easy to believe that wicked
men suffer for their sins; but it is difficult to find the reason for
good men suffering when they are good. From Job's experience

we learn that troubles may overwhelm the righteous, not as punishment for wrong, but as a test of their integrity.

In the land of Uz there lived a prosperous, godly man who loved his family and thanked the Lord for his blessings. He seemed to have security that would last for many years, but he was to learn that ruin can come swiftly. Job did not know how the divine plan was evolving, and all he could do was trust his heavenly Father. Now the good man had caught the attention of Satan, and the enemy of man appeared before God and challenged Job's religion. How many times our profession of Christianity is challenged today by men and women who say, "Let's see a genuine follower of Jesus Christ"? Can God testify of us as He did of Job: "Hast thou considered My servants, Neighbor Bradley or Dr. Freeman?"

Satan accused Job of doing right merely because of what he got in return. Job's piety was declared to be merely a matter of self-interest. The Lord said to Satan, "Behold, all that he has is in your power; only upon himself do not put forth your hand." Job 1:12, R.S.V. Even though the enemy may come upon us with his fierce attacks, it is comforting to know he can go no further than God permits.

The first blow was struck against Job's cattle and sheep and camels. These valuable possessions were swept away as in a moment. The second tragedy was the result of a tornado that wrecked the house where his sons and daughters were gathered, and killed all his children. Calamity was heaped on calamity!

In these tragic events Job did not sin or blame God for the trouble that befell him. The patient man might have asked, "Are all my prayers for my children in vain? Why would a loving God allow all these faithful young people to be taken away?"

As Robinson states, the messengers brought "crushing tidings for a father's ears. All dead, dead all at once—dead prematurely—dead by a sudden, unusual, and miserable death, dead as if by the hand of God Himself." Yet in this hour of staggering blows, Job held on to God.

Job was resigned to God's will, for he said, "The Lord gave, and the Lord hath taken away; blessed be the name of the Lord." Job 1:21. All of us must experience some form of resignation. Some must give up earthly happiness, some must be without love, some must renounce cherished hopes and plans. Resignation is not merely grinning and bearing it; it is accepting the divine will with good grace. Charles Lamb once paid this tribute to one who had suffered: "He gave his heart to the Purifier, and his will to the Sovereign Will of the universe." Only thus can we reach the experience described by Dante in the *Paradiso:* "In His will is our peace."

When Sickness Comes

Job's health was the next target of the evil one. A painful disease attacked the man, and he had no rest day or night, for in those days there was no sedative a physician could give that would lull the patient into slumber. The excruciating pain weakened Job and made him more susceptible to temptation.

See the sufferer, a man of prominence in his city, who is almost deserted by friends and loved ones. In those times, sickness was considered to be the curse of God, and men fled from it in fear. Job, who had once known the respect of young men and the honor of the aged, now says:

> "My kinsfolk and my close friends have failed me;
>   the guests in my house have forgotten me; . . .
> I am repulsive to my wife,
>   loathsome to the sons of my own mother."
>   Job 19:14-17, R.S.V.

To climax his troubles, Job's wife refused to stand by his side and encourage him. Scorning her husband's persistent faith, she said, "Do you still hold fast your integrity? Curse God, and die." Job 2:9, R.S.V. Gordon Chilvers makes this astute observation: "Satan had taken away Job's wealth, his children, and his health, but he did not take away his wife—her influence was used to make Job's trial greater. . . . The severity of this trial lay in this fact that the one who should have been his help and source of comfort in time of trial became his temptress and the tool of Satan."—*Moody Monthly,* July, 1953.

If ever a man might be justified for losing his temper it would be when Job's wife turned against him after he was saddled with the full burden of loss and grief! If ever a man seemed to have an excuse to flare up and shout angrily at his spouse, it was then. But the Bible states plainly: "In all this Job did not sin with his lips." Job 2:10, R.S.V. It would seem that the book of Job is asking again and again: "Is there such a thing as a sincere, wholehearted person who serves God just because it is the right thing to do?" And the life of Job proclaims the answer: "Yes!"

Troubles come to all of us, but they come without our choosing. We are not permitted to go to a store and select the "trouble" of our choice, and if it were possible none of us would be satisfied with our "bargain." No man would ever be willing to choose a trial or select his suffering.

Joseph Addison gives us a vivid lesson in his essay. He dreamed that the ruler of the world proclaimed that every person should bring his troubles and sorrows to a certain broad plain on a definite day. Humanity came like a vast army and piled their troubles high. Then a second order was given commanding everyone to choose another burden or trouble from the pile. The mortals rushed forward to make their choice, but they soon discovered that their new trouble was worse than their former one. Then, in the dream, the ruler of the world allowed each person to resume his own burden. When he had done so, the troubles of life seemed to shrink to about a third of their former size. With the help of our Saviour, our burdens grow lighter still and we can go forward, knowing that He cares for us.

The Test of False Philosophy

The next torturing ordeal that came to Job was the visit of his friends with their false accusations and distorted religious views. "Now when Job's three friends heard of all this evil that had come upon him, they came each from his own place. . . . And when they saw him from afar, they did not recognize him; and they raised their voices and wept; . . . and they sat with him on the ground seven days and seven nights, and no one spoke a word to him, for they saw that his suffering was very great." Verses 11-13, R.S.V.

Finally, Eliphaz led the round of arguments by asking Job, "Think now, who that was innocent ever perished? Or where were the upright cut off?" Job 4:7, R.S.V. In other words, it was plain to this friend that no innocent person ever reaped trouble or sorrow. He was attempting to show that God bestows happiness and prosperity in proportion to man's obedience. There was some defect of character, some secret sin in Job, so Eliphaz believed, that caused all this suffering. Zophar emphasized the same thought with these smug words: "Know then that God exacts of you less than your guilt deserves." Job 11:6, R.S.V.

Furthermore, the "comforters" told Job that death came to his children because of their evil-doing. Bildad said, "If your children have sinned against Him, He has delivered them into the power of their transgression." Job 8:4, R.S.V. These words must have cut like a knife into the heart of the patient sufferer, for he had brought his children up to have faith in God and to obey the divine commandments. Here Bildad assumed something for which there was no proof.

When the "friends" could not point to specific sin in Job's life, they began to surmise that he mistreated the poor and the orphans. Job 22:5-9. But by this time the sufferer had quit attempting to defend himself, for he cried out:

> "Oh, that I knew where I might find Him,
>   that I might come even to His seat!"
> "But He knows the way that I take;
>   when He has tried me, I shall come forth as gold."
>   Job 23:3, 10, R.S.V.

Now even saintly persons can be wrong in their thinking, and this was true when Job thought that his trouble was from God. He cried out:

> "For the arrows of the Almighty are in me;
>   my spirit drinks their poison;
>   the terrors of God are arrayed against me."
>   Job 6:4, R.S.V.

God had not shot the arrows of suffering at His faithful servant; but He had permitted the test to prove Job's integrity. Let us be certain that we do not blame God for what He never sends.

Were Job's friends correct in their philosophy of sin and suffering? They were religious men who were convinced that God deals out judgment according to a man's sin. They looked upon Job as proof of their belief, but they were wrong, woefully wrong. We read: "Job's professed friends were miserable com-

forters, making his case more bitter and unbearable, and Job
was not guilty as they supposed."—*Testimonies to Ministers,*
page 350.

The Voice of the Almighty

God steps into the drama through the Voice in the whirlwind, and He challenges puny man to answer the basic questions concerning creation and the wonders of the universe.
After some eighty-two questions have been propounded, none
of which Job can answer, the humble sufferer says:

> "Behold, I am of small account;
> what shall I answer Thee?
> I lay my hand on my mouth."
> Job 40:4, R.S.V.

The Almighty states plainly that the views of the three
friends are false. "My wrath is kindled against you and against
your two friends," God says to Eliphaz; "for you have not spoken of Me what is right, as My servant Job has." Job 42:7, R.S.V.

If Job was able to speak that which was acceptable to God, it
was because the man had knelt humbly on "the world's great
altar stairs which slope through darkness up to God." From
the despondency of the ash heap Job arose to mountain heights
of trust, for in the supreme moment we hear him exclaim,
"Though He slay me, yet will I trust Him."

Job was so pressed down by the burden of suffering and
calamity that he longed to weigh it on the scales. Job 6:2. But
there are no scales that can measure humanity's load of sorrow, for each one thinks his own is the heaviest. However, we
can be sure that the heavenly Father will allow no trial to come
that is greater than we can bear. And in the maelstrom of
suffering Job found divine power to keep him from ruin.

When the Almighty spoke from the whirlwind, Job and his friends stopped their arguments. There is a wonderful lesson for every Christian in this experience of listening to God. May we come to the same conclusion that Job reached when he said to God:

> "I know that Thou canst do all things,
> and that no purpose of Thine can be thwarted."
> Job 42:2, R.S.V.

Job's Captivity Ended

The testing fires of pain and sorrow were finally quenched. Although Job did not know it, he had outwitted the cunning of Satan and vindicated God's confidence in him. Job must have felt a wonderful peace, for he had "come forth as gold" through the help of the Spirit of God.

The three friends who had not spoken "what is right" were instructed to offer sacrifices to the Lord and to ask Job to pray for them. "And the Lord restored the fortunes of Job, when he had prayed for his friends; and the Lord gave Job twice as much as he had before." Job 42:10, R.S.V.

Long arguments and endless debates did not change the views of the three friends concerning religion; but Job's unwavering faith, consistent life, and prayers brought them to see their great need. Human nature has not changed, and today, even as in Job's generation, a godly life is the most powerful argument for the truth. "Not all the books written can serve the purpose of a holy life."—*Testimonies,* vol. 9, p. 21.

Job's patient endurance became the ideal of the Jewish people, and in the New Testament the apostle James writes to the church: "You have heard of the steadfastness of Job, and you have seen the purpose of the Lord, how the Lord is compassionate and merciful." James 5:11, R.S.V.

How changed our view of calamity and sorrow can be if we see "the purpose of the Lord." Our chief concern with the problem of suffering is not to find an explanation for it, but to find victory! "I do not want to die," wrote Katherine Mansfield, "without leaving a record of my belief that suffering can be overcome. For I do believe it. Everything in life that we really accept undergoes a change. So suffering becomes love."

If Paul and Job could have recounted their tribulations, the physical pain, their bitter treatment by others, I am sure they would have joined in saying, "In all these things we are more than conquerors through Him that loved us." Romans 8:37.

"It is precisely from the company of the sons and daughters of affliction that the most convinced believers of all the ages have sprung. Who are the men whose names stand on the dramatic roll call of the faithful in Hebrews? Are they men whose days were happy and unclouded and serene, souls for whom the sun was always shining and the skies unvisited by storm or midnight? If anyone imagines that such is the background of faith, let him listen to this—'They were stoned, they were sawn asunder, were tempted, were slain with the sword, destitute, afflicted, tormented; they wandered in deserts, and in mountains, and in dens and caves of the earth.' That, declares the New Testament, has been in every age faith's grim heredity! And it is not from sheltered ways and quiet, sequestered paths, it is from a thousand crosses, that the cry ascends—'Hallelujah! For the Lord God omnipotent reigneth.'"—James S. Stewart, *The Strong Name,* page 153.

WHY JESUS SUFFERED

∽5∽

"A Man of Sorrows"

JESUS CHRIST is our Example in all things, even in suffering. He did not seek martyrdom, neither did He run away from it. He understood suffering to be an appointed means of accomplishing His Father's will, and when it came upon Him like a flood, He was able to pray, "Thy will be done."

Our Saviour was not triumphant in suffering because of His divine nature. No, He laid aside all of heaven's glory and took all the weakness of humanity, even "the seed of Abraham" and the body of our humiliation. As a weak human being He knew all about the pain, the disappointment, the trials and sorrows that mankind faces. Jesus can sympathize with humanity's suffering in a way no other being in the universe will ever know, for He spent nights in prayer; He felt hunger, pain, mental torture, fatigue, discouragement, and despair.

In Jesus we have the supreme example of vicarious suffering. There are occasions when men have taken the penalty of a crime for a friend or loved one; but while mankind was at enmity against God, Jesus came and suffered and died—not to save Himself but that we might have eternal life. The Son of man fasted forty days and when physically depleted was tempted of the devil; He suffered ignominy and shame; He faced the terrors of death in Gethsemane and longed to escape them; He took the mocking and ridicule of pagan soldiers and hypocritical Jewish leaders, and finally He died on Calvary. Why? He did all of this for one purpose—to save us from sin. His pure heart felt the degradation, the guilt, and the utter lost condition of the sinner in order that He might know how to enter into the experience of every man and faithfully intercede for him in heaven's tribunal.

The vicarious suffering of Jesus is portrayed in Isaiah's prophecy, where we see the suffering Servant bowing under man's horrible burden of woe. In all our "affliction He was afflicted." Isaiah 63:9. The sorrows He endured were ours, not His. "Surely He has borne *our* griefs and carried *our* sorrows; . . . He was wounded for *our* transgressions, He was bruised for *our* iniquities." Isaiah 53:4, 5, R.S.V.

The Pathway of Suffering

If today we could have a clear and reasonable explanation of all pain and suffering, that would be of little help in our dire need. We must have grace and help to bear it. *This is why Jesus suffered*. To be a perfect and faithful representative of man, Jesus Christ must know how humanity has been tortured by sin. "Therefore He had to be made like His brethren in every respect, so that He might become a merciful and faithful high priest in the service of God, to make expiation for the sins of the people." Hebrews 2:17, R.S.V.

If Jesus could not have sinned He could not have been tempted. A man who is blind cannot be tempted to see evil pictures. We can be tempted only because we are able to succumb to sin. Therefore, "because He Himself has suffered and been tempted, He is able to help those who are tempted." Hebrews 2:18, R.S.V. This means that He knew the pull of

4—T.S.

sin, He knew tragic disappointment, loss, and pain; but He came through it all triumphantly.

For our sake God "made Him to be sin for us, who knew no sin." 2 Corinthians 5:21. The Saviour never yielded to temptation; therefore, He did not know sin as the result of His own evil-doing. However, He took on Himself the entire burden of sin—the shame, the suffering, and the judgment of God. Thus He was made "sin" for us.

"If we had to bear anything which Jesus did not endure, then upon this point Satan would represent the power of God as insufficient for us. Therefore Jesus was 'in all points tempted like as we are.' Hebrews 4:15. He endured every trial to which we are subject. And He exercised in His own behalf no power that is not freely offered to us. As man, He met temptation, and overcame in the strength given Him from God."—*The Desire of Ages,* page 24.

Obedience Through Suffering

Many a person has gone on in a defiant, headstrong way until suffering caused him to bow his head and seek God's will. Jesus Christ did not defy His Father's will, or rebel against the divine plan, but He did learn the way of perfect obedience as the result of suffering. "Although He was a Son, He learned obedience through what He suffered." Hebrews 5:8, R.S.V.

At no point in His earthly life did Jesus turn aside from His Father's plan. At the age of twelve years He said, "I must be about My Father's business." Luke 2:49. To His disciples Jesus declared His purpose in these words: "My meat is to do the will of Him that sent Me, and to finish His work." John 4:34. In Gethsemane the Saviour prayed, "Nevertheless not *My* will, but Thine, be done." Luke 22:42. And His obedience

led Him to humiliation and death, "even death on a cross."
Philippians 2:8, R.S.V.

If sorrow and trial are necessary to bring us to obedience,
then let us welcome the ordeal. The Son of God learned perfectly all that the right use of suffering can teach us. And He
says, "My child, trust and obey. Out of this suffering can come
the sublime lesson that you need."

The Love Supreme

From the first moments of hunger in the wilderness of
temptation until He cried, "I thirst," as He hung on the cross,
Jesus endured much physical pain. He knew the brutality of
Roman soldiers as they scourged Him, spat upon Him, and
placed a crown of thorns on His head. He fell beneath the
weight of the cross, and He felt the searing pain of nails driven
into His sensitive hands and feet. In the hours of darkness on
the cross His feverish body and tortured muscles found no
surcease from pain. And then Jesus knew the agony of death.
Why did He suffer? There is only one answer, and the apostle
Peter states it bluntly: "Christ hath suffered for us in the flesh."
1 Peter 4:1. Yes, we were the cause for all His suffering, and
"with His stripes we are healed."

Let no suffering child of God say that our heavenly Father
does not love us. He poured out His heart for us through the
suffering of His Son. Jesus shielded us from the penalty of sin
because He loved us. An illustration of the length of human
love that is a faint shadow of how Christ loves us is related by
Dr. W. Russell Maltby in *The Meaning of the Cross:*

There was "a workingman in the North of England whose
wife, soon after her marriage, drifted into vicious ways, and
went rapidly from bad to worse. He came home one Sunday
evening to find, as he had found a dozen times before, that

she had gone on a new debauch. He knew in what condition she would return, after two or three days of a nameless life. He sat down in the cheerless house to look the truth in the face and to find what he must do. The worst had happened too often to leave him with much hope, and he saw in part what was in store for him. Now that a new and terrible meaning had passed into the words 'for better, for worse,' he reaffirmed his marriage vow. Later, when someone who knew them both intimately, ventured to commiserate him, he answered, 'Not a word! She is my wife, and I shall love her as long as there is breath in my body.' She did not mend, and died in his house after some years in a shameful condition, with his hands spread over her in pity and in prayer."

This is a feeble illustration of how our Lord, the Bridegroom and Husband of His church, has loved us with an everlasting love, even when we sank into the pit of sin. "Christ has shown that His love was stronger than death. He was accomplishing man's salvation; and although He had the most fearful conflict with the powers of darkness, yet, amid it all, His love grew stronger and stronger."—*Testimonies,* vol. 2, p. 212.

But the physical, outward ordeal of the Christ was only a symbol of the deeper spiritual suffering. Jesus was lonely, misunderstood, and rejected by the majority of those He came to save. He suffered the agony of rejection because sinners were blind to their need of salvation and they spurned the love of God manifest in His Son. We can never comprehend the Master's sorrow as He looked upon Jerusalem, the city that was turning its back upon Him and plotting to crucify Him.

"It was the sight of Jerusalem that pierced the heart of Jesus—Jerusalem that had rejected the Son of God and scorned His love, that refused to be convinced by His mighty miracles, and was about to take His life. He saw what she was in her guilt of rejecting her Redeemer, and what she might have been had she accepted Him who alone could heal her wound. He had come to save her; how could He give her up?"—*The Desire of Ages,* page 576.

The supreme portrayal of divine love is seen on Golgotha's cross where the Lamb of God was made sin for us. His greatest suffering was to be shut away from His Father. Hear His cry: "My God, My God, why hast Thou forsaken Me?"

"Sorrow is the consciousness of lack," says G. Campbell Morgan. "What is the sorrow of sickness but the consciousness of lack of health? What is the sorrow of bereavement but the consciousness of the lack of the loved one? . . . What is the sorrow of loneliness but the consciousness of the lack of companionship? All sorrow is lack. Then it follows by a natural sequence of thought, that the uttermost depth of sorrow is lack of God. There is no sorrow like it."—*The Crises of the Christ,* pages 299, 300.

Jesus experienced the agonizing despair of the lost sinner separated from God by an impassable gulf. This is the greatest suffering ever witnessed in the universe. It is the supreme demonstration of love!

The Fellowship of Christ's Sufferings

The privilege of sharing in Christ's sufferings was a blessed comfort to the apostle Paul in his trials and persecutions. To the church in Corinth, he wrote, "For as we share abundantly in Christ's sufferings, so through Christ we share abundantly in comfort too." 2 Corinthians 1:5, R.S.V. When Paul suffered for his faith as he ministered to the churches, he knew he was walking in the steps of his Master.

We, too, share the sufferings of our Lord when we take up our cross and follow Him. First of all, we can return to

Gethsemane and Golgotha and meditate upon heaven's sacrifice for us. "It would be well for us to spend a thoughtful hour each day in contemplation of the life of Christ. We should take it point by point, and let the imagination grasp each scene, especially the closing ones. As we thus dwell upon His great sacrifice for us, our confidence in Him will be more constant, our love will be quickened, and we shall be more deeply imbued with His spirit. If we would be saved at last, we must learn the lesson of penitence and humiliation at the foot of the cross."—*The Desire of Ages,* page 83.

There are particular elements in suffering where we have fellowship with Jesus Christ. He suffered because of the sins of others; He felt the degradation and the awful consequences of sin in a way the sinner never could. For example, a parent suffers in the same way, but to a lesser degree, for a son or daughter who becomes a drug addict. The child may think lightly of his evil course, but the parent's love and deeper knowledge of all that is involved make his suffering the greater.

Jesus was not indifferent to human grief. He wept when He saw Martha and Mary grieving at their brother's tomb. While hanging upon the cross, the Son of God was touched by the sorrow of the women who stood nearby. "Although full of suffering, while bearing the sins of the world, He was not indifferent to the expression of grief. He looked upon these women with tender compassion."—*The Desire of Ages,* page 743. As His followers, we share His suffering when we "weep with them that weep," and sympathize with those who pass through the valley of the shadow.

Many times we suffer when we are obeying God's will. We may be hated, reviled, and persecuted; but in this dark hour we experience fellowship with Christ, for He deserved none of the suffering that was His lot.

When we walk with Jesus our sufferings are His sufferings, our sorrow is His sorrow. We can receive the greatest comfort and blessing as we know God is with us in all our trials and afflictions. James S. Stewart declares, "It is as though God said, in the day of darkness, 'Here, My child, is something you can do for Me! Here is your little share in the burden which I have been carrying from the foundation of the world and must carry till the day break and the shadows flee. Here is your part with Me in the age-long cross I bear.' "—*The Strong Name,* page 165.

> All those who journey, soon or late,
> Must pass within the garden's gate;
> Must kneel alone in darkness there,
> And battle with some fierce despair.
> God pity those who cannot say:
> "Not mine but Thine;" who only pray:
> "Let this cup pass," and cannot see
> The purpose in Gethsemane.
> —Ella Wheeler Wilcox.

Here is a new concept of suffering of which the world knows nothing. The Christian takes up his cross—a little share in the cross of Jesus—and bears the pain, sorrow, and tribulation, knowing he is in fellowship with his Master. Jesus is in it with us, and we are in it with Him. "And of all the gifts that heaven can bestow upon men, fellowship with Christ in His sufferings is the most weighty trust and the highest honor."—*The Desire of Ages,* page 225.

WE ARE NOT ALONE

~6~

God Is With Us in Suffering

FROM my own limited experience I agree with C. S. Lewis that "when pain is to be borne, a little courage helps more than knowledge, a little human sympathy more than much courage, and the least tincture of the love of God more than all."—*The Problem of Pain,* page viii.

It requires courage to face suffering at any time; but it takes all the fortitude a brave soul can muster to accept trial and affliction *alone,* without a friend or loved one to share the burden. Faith has ebbed from many a great man's soul when he was forced to fight alone.

Elijah, the militant prophet of Carmel, could defy the false religion of four hundred and fifty priests of Baal; but when he stood alone against the world and one woman's threatening, he was seized with panic fear. Elijah left his servant behind and ran until he was exhausted. As he sat under a tree he moaned, "It is enough; now, O Lord, take away my life; for I am no better than my fathers." 1 Kings 19:4, R.S.V.

Forty days later the prophet was found hiding in a desert cave near Mount Sinai, and fearfully he told the Lord: "I, even I only, am left; and they seek my life, to take it away." Verse

10. The prophet of God suffered deep mental anguish, for he believed that all he had struggled to win for the truth had been lost. He was without companionship or sympathy. "I am the only one left." "I *only* am left." This was his lamentation in loneliness. Yet, when Elijah was the most despondent, God came to His servant. Not in the storm, the earthquake, or fire did the message of love come; but in "a still small voice." The prophet was challenged to go forward on a special mission which took away his sorrow and loneliness. He was assured that he was not the only faithful follower of the true God, for there were seven thousand in Israel who had not worshiped Baal.

With new strength and vigor Elijah arose above his defeat and went forth a dedicated messenger of the Lord. "As the rock never appears more majestic than when seen standing alone, with the ocean billows rolling round it, so with one who is 'faithful found among the faithless,' cut off from all natural and human supports, isolated in a surrounding sea of indifference or iniquity."—*The Pulpit Commentary,* vol. 5, p. 474 (1 Kings 19:1-18).

David is another Old Testament figure who knew abject defeat and loneliness. His mental suffering must have been intense as he felt himself to be a "forgotten man." Psalms 10:1; 13:1. Yet the Lord of heaven was at his side to encourage him, and when his strength was renewed the psalmist could sing, "I will fear no evil: for Thou art with me." Psalm 23:4. When isolated by enemies, he could feel God's protection, for he said, "The angel of the Lord encampeth round about them that fear Him, and delivereth them." Psalm 34:7.

"If, under trying circumstances, men of spiritual power, pressed beyond measure, become discouraged and desponding; if at times they see nothing desirable in life, that they should choose it, this is nothing strange or new. . . . When we are encompassed with doubt, perplexed by circumstances, or afflicted by poverty or distress, Satan seeks to shake our confidence in Jehovah. . . . Abiding in God's love, you may stand every test."—*Prophets and Kings,* pages 173-175.

The Loneliness of the Master

Every human being desires to fit into his environment; he longs to be understood and accepted. It was the bitter cup of loneliness and misunderstanding that Jesus Christ drank throughout His earthly life. In childhood His playmates and brothers misunderstood Him. The Saviour mingled with the crowds in city or on the hillside, "yet through childhood, youth, and manhood, Jesus walked alone. In His purity and His faithfulness, He trod the wine press alone, and of the people there was none with Him."—*The Desire of Ages,* page 92.

After His baptism the Son of man went into the desert and for forty days experienced deepest solitude. No faithful companion shared His anguish of soul, no human helper was beside Him in the ordeal of temptation. Later Jesus called twelve disciples to follow Him, but even they could not fully appreciate His work. "Throughout His life His mother and His brothers did not comprehend His mission. Even His disciples did not understand Him. . . . Alone He must tread the path; alone He must bear the burden."—*Ibid.,* p. 111.

When human companionship failed Him, Jesus went to His Father in prayer. The climax of temptation came in the Garden of Gethsemane. In His humanity He asked His sleeping disciples in the garden, "What, could ye not watch with Me one hour?" Although the fate of all mankind hung in the balance, the uncomprehending disciples slept on while Jesus suffered alone! When soldiers came to take Jesus, the disciples were afraid, and "they all forsook Him, and fled." The Son of God, who had enjoyed the adoration of angels and the fellowship of heavenly beings, was deserted by His followers in His trial, scourging, and crucifixion. The Saviour knew that men would desert Him, for He had prophesied: "Behold, the hour cometh, yea, is now come, that ye shall be scattered, every man to his own, and shall leave Me alone: and yet I am not alone, because the Father is with Me." John 16:32. This was the secret of the Master's strength, and it is the source of power for every Christian today.

"Whatever our distress, we can be sure that God sees us and that God cares for us," says Clarence E. Macartney. "If ever we are tempted to cry out with the psalmist, 'No man cared for my soul,' let us remember that God cares for us and that His providence is over us. As Jeremy Taylor, the master of English style, once put it, 'We are safer in God's storm, with God present, than we are in the calm of the world.' Whatever our difficulties, let us have faith that God will open our eyes and that we shall see, as Hagar saw in the wilderness, a well of water springing up for our refreshment. We can answer every temptation to doubt and despair, every assault of the world and of the devil, with that beautiful confession of faith by the slave girl there in the lonely wilderness: 'Thou God seest me.' "

But the Son of God must go farther into suffering than any sinner will ever be called to go. Not only did Jesus face Pilate, Herod, the Roman soldiers, and the mob alone, but He died on the cross, shut away from His Father. While He suffered physical torture He knew greater mental anguish as He was reviled and mocked. He listened for some word of courage from His disciples that would reveal their faith; but they were silent. The only moment of comfort came to the Son of God when the thief asked for salvation; Christ promised him eternal life, though His own valley of the shadow was just ahead. All that He heard from the crowd was the sound of curses and jeers.

When the final dark hour came, the Father shut Himself completely from His Son. There was no comfort, no hope, no promise, for the dying Lord of heaven and earth! "The sins of the world were upon Him, also the sense of His Father's wrath as He suffered the penalty of the law transgressed. It was these that crushed His divine soul. It was the hiding of His Father's face—a sense that His own dear Father had forsaken Him—which brought despair. The separation that sin makes between God and man was fully realized and keenly felt by the innocent, suffering Man of Calvary. He was oppressed by the powers of darkness. He had not one ray of light to brighten the future."—*Testimonies,* vol. 2, p. 214.

> Though long the weary way we tread,
>   And sorrow crown each lingering year,
> No path we shun, no darkness dread,
>   Our hearts still whispering, Thou art near!
>
> When drooping pleasure turns to grief,
>   And trembling faith is changed to fear,
> The murmuring wind, the quivering leaf,
>   Shall softly tell us, Thou art near!
>   —Oliver Wendell Holmes.

No child of God will ever be called to drink the lonely cup of grief our Saviour accepted. He felt that the whole race of men had betrayed, deserted, or rejected Him, and there was no one to understand the poignancy of His grief.

Clarence E. Macartney has said, "Because Christ tasted that loneliness for us and drank our cup, no soul need ever remain in the lonely night and darkness of sin. Peter, too, sinned and went out into the night and wept bitterly, but he did not forget that look which Jesus gave him when He heard him cursing and denying that he ever knew Him. It was that look that brought him to repentance and gave him forgiveness. Are you lonely because of sin? Then that is the cure for you, that loving, yearning, forgiving look of that wonderful Saviour who loved you and gave Himself for you."—*You Can Conquer,* page 55.

God Stood Beside Paul

It was the thought that Jesus Christ had been triumphant in suffering that sustained the apostles through trial, imprisonment, and martyrdom in the early history of the church. When Paul was in prison in Rome he knew something of his Saviour's lonely vigil. To Timothy the imprisoned apostle wrote, "At my first defense no one took my part; all deserted me." 2 Timothy 4:16, R.S.V. But the next verse reveals the valiant warrior of the cross in all his fortitude, as he says, "But the Lord stood by me and gave me strength to proclaim the word fully, that all the Gentiles might hear it." Verse 17, R.S.V. Pagan, sophisticated Romans looked skeptically at this prisoner from Jerusalem. There was no friend or fellow Christian in the court at his trial. Yet in that heartbreaking hour Jesus Christ stood by his side, and Paul rejoiced.

How changed is the suffering we must endure when we know Jesus is by our side! When the three Hebrew worthies were thrown into the red-hot furnace, they were not alone. A fourth person was walking in the fire with them! "As His witnesses were cast into the furnace, the Saviour revealed Himself to them in person, and together they walked in the midst of the fire."—*Prophets and Kings,* pages 508, 509.

In a world bent and almost broken by pain, affliction, and

disillusionment, the Christian can be a comforter. God "comforts us in all our affliction, so that we may be able to comfort those who are in any affliction, with the comfort with which we ourselves are comforted by God." 2 Corinthians 1:4, R.S.V. There is a blessing in suffering we may not as yet have found— it can prepare us to be a sympathetic helper to those in sorrow and pain. We need compassion and sympathy such as Jesus had, for His heart of love went out to every poor, struggling soul.

We will never be able to enter fully into the sufferings of our brother man as Jesus did; but there is a sense in which we can follow His steps as we help lift the burdens and speak the word of cheer. "Suffering in which we have found for ourselves the comfort of God is an equipment for service. It puts us alongside of others. It gives us entry to their pain, making them willing to listen to us. We can speak with authority for we have been there."—*The Interpreter's Bible,* vol. 10, p. 281.

The Master's Commission

As Jesus met with His disciples after His resurrection, He found them afraid that the Jews would kill them. How comforting was the Master's assurance: "Peace be unto you." At that moment He gave them a definite commission: "As My Father hath sent Me, even so send I you." John 20:21.

The Son of God proclaimed His mission to men when He preached His first sermon in Nazareth, for He said:

"The Spirit of the Lord is upon Me,
    because He has anointed Me to preach good news to the poor.
He has sent Me to proclaim release to the captives
    and recovering of sight to the blind,
    to set at liberty those who are oppressed,
    to proclaim the acceptable year of the Lord."
                         Luke 4:18, 19, R.S.V.

The same royal service of love has been entrusted to everyone who takes the name of Christ and follows Him. We are called to help the poor, the oppressed, the suffering, and heartbroken. "Never should we pass by one suffering soul without seeking to impart to him of the comfort wherewith we are comforted of God."—*The Desire of Ages,* page 505.

There are many lonely hearts who have never met Jesus Christ or learned to love Him. In their solitude and suffering they need our assistance, and through us they may find the Saviour. We can tell them of His peace that passeth understanding.

"Through all our trials we have a never-failing Helper. He does not leave us alone to struggle with temptation, to battle with evil, and be finally crushed with burdens and sorrow. Though now He is hidden from mortal sight, the ear of faith can hear His voice saying, Fear not; I am with you. 'I am He that liveth, and was dead; and, behold, I am alive for evermore.' Revelation 1:18. I have endured your sorrows, experienced your struggles, encountered your temptations. I know your tears; I also have wept. The griefs that lie too deep to be breathed into any human ear, I know. Think not that you are desolate and forsaken. Though your pain touch no responsive chord in any heart on earth, look unto Me, and live."—*The Desire of Ages,* page 483.

Thank God, we are not alone in this chaotic world. "There is a Friend that sticketh closer than a brother." Proverbs 18:24. The apostle Peter knew what Jesus had done for him, and he admonishes us to "cast all your anxieties on Him, for He cares about you." 1 Peter 5:7, R.S.V. Have you proved His love and found His comfort in your life?

THE SEARCH FOR GOLD

∽7∽

God's Purpose in Suffering

WHEN we surrender our will to God and follow His blueprint, living unselfishly in a selfish world, striving for purity in a corrupt generation, we are certain to have trials and troubles. This does not mean that the Christian flaunts his religion or deliberately walks into trouble, but he finds he is thrust into the same world of sin that rejected and crucified his Lord. James asks, "Know ye not that the friendship of the world is enmity with God? whosoever therefore will be a friend of the world is the enemy of God." James 4:4. Jesus never promised His followers a calm, untroubled existence in a world antagonistic to His message, for He said, "In the world you have tribulation; but be of good cheer, I have overcome the world." John 16:33, R.S.V.

Therefore suffering should be regarded as a normal part of the Christian's life. It is neither unusual nor strange. Many persons live to the sad strains of suffering; it is the dominant minor melody. Because of this fact, the apostle James makes the daring statement: "Greet it as pure joy, my brothers, when you encounter any sort of trial." James 1:2, Moffatt. Yes, the Christian is to accept the trials and afflictions seriously, willingly, and also *joyfully.*

(56)

The word *tribulation* means "to press or afflict." The ancient *tribulum* was a threshing sledge; therefore tribulation is related to the process of threshing grain, separating it from the chaff. For the Christian, tribulation may be necessary to beat out the worthless and cherish the rich grain of character.

The Fruits of Suffering

Rightly accepted, the experience of suffering does not destroy our faith; it strengthens it and causes the follower of Christ to bring forth fruit. The writer of the book of Hebrews tells us: "For the moment all discipline seems painful rather than pleasant; later it yields the peaceful fruit of righteousness to those who have been trained by it." Hebrews 12:11, R.S.V.

Suffering and trial are required courses in the college of Christlike living. If we are "trained" by hardship and pain we will be humble and teachable. If we refuse the course of study and turn away, we will become embittered and ignorant of God's plan for us.

Patience is a noble virtue that develops through a lifetime. No one ever saw a patient baby, for no one is born with patience. James says, "Let patience have her perfect work, that ye may be perfect and entire, wanting nothing." James 1:4. This is the kind of patience John Wesley's mother possessed. One day her husband asked her, "How could you have the patience to tell that blockhead son the same thing twenty times?"

"If I had told him but nineteen times," she quietly replied, "I should have lost all my labor."

"None who receive God's word are exempt from difficulty and trial; but when affliction comes, the true Christian does not become restless, distrustful, or despondent. Though we cannot see the definite outcome of affairs, or discern the purpose of God's providences, we are not to cast away our confidence. Remembering the tender mercies of the Lord, we should cast our care upon Him, and with patience wait for His salvation."—*Christ's Object Lessons,* pages 60, 61.

These are days when the tension becomes great and tempers are short. It is a time for "the patience of the saints" to be manifest. Enduring suffering and hardship with a calm, sweet spirit is an evidence of patience.

Clara Barton once advised her young niece to be patient. "Keep yourself quiet and in restraint," she said. "Reserve your energies doing those little things that lie in your way, each one as well as you can, saving your strength, so that when God does call you to do something good and great, you will not have wasted your force and strength with useless strivings, but will do the work quickly and well."

A patient man and an impatient one may both lose heavily on the stock market, or both of them may come down with the same disease. The trouble might be as near alike as could come to two humans, but the reaction of the two men will be vastly different. Why? Because of the strength of character in the patient man and the lack of stabiliy and fortitude in the other. Life's values can often be determined more by *reactions* than by mere actions.

Patience means more than passively accepting trial and difficulty. Patience suggests endurance, waiting for something to happen, for someone to help. "The patience of the saints" is an *active* experience; it is the certain belief that God will stand by His suffering child and give him strength to endure.

Accepting pain and suffering in the right spirit helps to draw man back to God. "The finest men and women have recognized the part played by suffering in the making of noble character and the achievement of human usefulness," says

James W. Wilson. " 'In the story of the great, one chapter is invariably entitled "Pain." ' Pain is one of God's hardest-to-accept means of transforming and redeeming a human life." —*Religion in Life,* vol. 19, p. 168.

The famous violinist Ole Bull was once giving a concert at Munich when his A string snapped. Without hesitation he finished the program by playing on three strings. How like the undaunted Christian, who, when handicapped by sickness or adversity, learns to get life's music from the strings he has left! There was John Milton, writing his most magnificent poetry after he was blind; Ludwig van Beethoven composing his richest sonatas when deafness had overtaken him. Nor can we forget the spirit of Louis Pasteur, who made his scientific discoveries after a paralytic stroke had crippled him at the age of forty-six.

Yes, pain and suffering, rightly used, have developed greatness in men because they allowed it to bring forth the precious gold of character. Disappointed hopes became the challenge to do great things for God and for the love of fellow men.

The psalmist recognized how sorrow could draw a soul to the path of right, for he said, "Before I was afflicted I went astray: but now have I kept Thy word." Psalm 119:67. Some of life's profoundest lessons have been learned in a hospital bed, in an iron lung, in a wheel chair, or in prison. The "suffering is not good in itself," C. S. Lewis points out. "What is good in any painful experience is, for the sufferer, his submission to the will of God, and for the spectators, the compassion aroused and the acts of mercy to which it leads."—*The Problem of Pain,* page 98.

We Are Not Judges

Let us agree, then, that a loving God is not in the pain, the sorrow, the dying, and the myriad tragedies of daily account.

These are all evil in themselves; yet out of the grief, the agony, and the suffering may come the gold of a Christlike character. It has been refined in the crucible of affliction.

No man has a right to be a judge over his fellow men in matters of suffering. Sometimes we hear shallow-minded persons say something like this: "The death of her husband came because she left the church." Or, "He has been stricken with that disease because he wasn't faithful to God." Such was the distorted thinking of many persons in Christ's time, for the Jews considered all sickness and pain to be punishment in this life for some wrongdoing.

Jesus exploded this fallacy when He healed the man born blind. The disciples asked Jesus, "Who did sin, this man, or his parents, that he was born blind?"

"Neither hath this man sinned, nor his parents: but that the works of God should be made manifest in him." John 9:2, 3.

Jesus healed the blind man—a direct answer to the questioning disciples. They "were not called upon to discuss the question as to who had sinned or had not sinned, but to understand the power and mercy of God in giving sight to the blind."— *The Desire of Ages,* page 471.

In commenting upon this experience of Jesus, *The Expositor's Bible* makes an excellent observation: "It was our Lord's intention to warn the disciples against a curious and uncharitable scrutiny of any man's life to find the cause of his misfortunes. We have to do rather with the future than with the past, rather with the question how we can help the man out of his difficulties than with the question how he got himself into them. . . . No matter what has caused the suffering, here certainly it is always with us, and what we have to do with it is to find in it material and opportunity for a work of God."— Vol. 5, pp. 180, 181.

Think what a load was lifted that day from the blind man and from his parents when Jesus answered, "Neither hath this man sinned, nor his parents." No doubt the parents had endured years of mental anguish, trying to search their souls for the sin that had caused the baby to be born blind. Now they were clear of blame.

In like manner let us remember this divine lesson when men and women suffer today, for much of it comes through no direct fault of their own. Let us leave the mystery to God and refrain from judging when we do not have, and cannot obtain, the evidence.

Dr. Arthur J. Gossip says, "No doubt at all, sin does have penal consequences; and sometimes some of them are physical. Any doctor will tell us that this very case of blindness from birth is sometimes the direct result of the father's or the mother's misdemeanors. Sometimes. But there are many other possibilities that may account for such catastrophes; and to read the sinister interpretation into every case would be monstrously unjust."—*The Interpreter's Bible,* vol. 8, p. 612.

A Test for Eternity

The fires of adversity can be the testing to prepare us for the final crisis. Faith is essential today, even as it was in the time of Abraham. Faith holds on when there is no human way out of the darkness. When we think of faith our minds turn to Hebrews 11:1. New light has recently been thrown on the word from the Greek which is translated "substance." According to Bruce M. Metzger, the verse might well be rendered: "Now faith is the *title deed* of things hoped for." The Greek words have been found in business documents and contracts and refer to the possession of a piece of property. By faith we have the title deed to our heavenly home, and if we are ready to meet Jesus Christ when He appears, we will receive the reward. The fruits of the Spirit must be developed in every child of God *now* if he expects to stand the final test. "Many who profess the name of Christ and claim to be looking for His speedy coming, know not what it is to suffer for Christ's sake."—*Early Writings,* page 113.

Some professed Christians suffer, not for the sake of the gospel, but because of their selfish, unregenerate hearts. They are tortured because they want to hold on to the world with one hand and to Jesus Christ with the other. The attempt to compromise brings only frustration and unhappiness.

The surrendered life gives up to God's plan, and when suffering comes, the Christian prays that it will better prepare him to meet his Saviour. Have you suffered? Remember Jesus climbed Golgotha's hill and His hands and feet were pierced for you. Have you been discouraged? Our Saviour saw the last ray of hope fade and darkness settle over the earth. We are told to expect suffering for the sake of our faith in Jesus. The disciples heard the Master say that enemies of truth would "lay their hands on you and persecute you, delivering you up to the synagogues and prisons, and you will be brought before kings and governors for My name's sake. This will be a time for you to bear testimony." Luke 21:12, 13, R.S.V.

In time of persecution, torture, and sorrow we are called to witness to the love of Jesus! Never was a testimony for Christianity of greater value than in periods of suffering and tragedy. This is the greatest proof that our faith in God is genuine. In such an ordeal the Master has promised to be at the side of His faithful follower. "Never is the tempest-tried soul more dearly loved by his Saviour than when he is suffering reproach for the truth's sake. 'I will love him,' Christ said, 'and

will manifest Myself to him.' When for the truth's sake the
believer stands at the bar of earthly tribunals, Christ stands by
his side."—*The Acts of the Apostles,* page 85.

The experience of suffering will not destroy the faith of
a genuine Christian; it strengthens it. There is a Swedish
proverb that says, "Blessed is he who sees a dawn in every
midnight." When suffering comes crashing in upon us and
we have exhausted our resources, then we surrender to God's
sustaining mercy and our hearts reach out for His love. The
very trials that make us feel deserted are the ones that can
draw us closer to Christ. As we come near with tear-filled eyes
we lay our burdens at His feet, and in exchange we receive
comfort and strength.

Will It Make "Brave Reading"?

Wonderful is the promise stated by the apostle James:
"Blessed is the man that endureth temptation: for when he is
tried, he shall receive the crown of life, which the Lord hath
promised to them that love Him." James 1:12.

Listen to the words of men and women who have endured
the test and come forth as gold: Esther in the palace casts her
lot with her doomed people as she says, "If I perish, I perish."
Esther 4:16. Joseph, faced with sinister temptation, exclaims,
"How then can I do this great wickedness, and sin against
God?" Genesis 39:9, R.S.V. Peter and his fellow apostles face
a council that recently voted to put the Son of God to death,
and the apostle says, "We must obey God rather than men."
Acts 5:29, R.S.V. Martin Luther defies the emperor with his
ringing testimony: "Here I stand. I can do no other; may God
help me. Amen."

It was this same Martin Luther who, in a severe illness and
writhing in pain, said, "These pains and troubles here are like

the type the printers set; as they look now, we have to read them backward, and they seem to have no sense or meaning in them; but yonder, when the Lord prints us off in the life to come, we shall find they make brave reading."

The testing will come, for everyone has a date with trials and adversity. Let us remember that Jesus Christ sees in us something worth developing, for He would not waste time on that which is of no value. "The Lord allows His chosen ones to be placed in the furnace of affliction, to prove what temper they are of, and whether they can be fashioned for His work."—*The Ministry of Healing,* page 471.

May we endure the testing and come forth as pure gold!

BEYOND THE SHADOWS

∼∘8∘∼

The Christian's Hope

IN A famous art gallery of Europe is a statue bearing the title, "The First Death." The sculptor has portrayed a mother holding the lifeless form of her son in her arms, while at her side stands the boy's father, a look of bewildering sorrow on his countenance. This may specifically represent the suffering of Adam and Eve over the death of Abel; but it also represents the universal loss that overwhelms us as we stand by the open grave of a loved one!

"I wish someone would light up the way for me," pleaded John Burroughs. When the grim shadows hover about us, we long for a ray of light that will give safe footing on the path ahead, for we are lonely and lost. With tears in her eyes a mother tells us that no amount of money could reimburse her for the loss of her son. Precious companionship and enduring love can never be measured by houses and lands or replaced with gold.

In the time of trouble it is the most natural thing for man to appeal to the Supreme Being. David said, "I stretch out my hands to Thee." Psalm 143:6, R.S.V. The answer is certain: "For this God is our God for ever and ever: He will be our Guide even unto death." Psalm 48:14.

No matter how involved we are in trouble or how great our perplexity, the Eternal One is our strong tower forever. Our Father's "watchcare extends to every household and encircles every individual; He is concerned in all our business and our sorrows. He marks every tear; He is touched with the feeling of our infirmities."—*Testimonies,* vol. 5, p. 742.

The key to the mystery of death is found in the radiant words: "He is risen." The resurrection of Jesus is the triumph of Christianity, for He not only defeated death on that memorable morning He came from the tomb; but He is alive forever, and He is our resurrection and life. The apostle Peter called his Lord "the Pioneer of Life." Acts 3:14, Moffatt. Through our Saviour the life that was forfeited in Eden because of sin was regained for the human race when He broke the seal on the tomb.

We can see light in the valley of the shadow because the Son of God has passed through it.

> Christ leads me through no darker rooms
> Than He went through before.

Today the glorified Son of God proclaims, "I am the resurrection and the life; he who believes in Me, though he die, yet shall he live." John 11:25, R.S.V. No comment upon these glorious words is adequate. Indeed the message is beyond human comprehension, and all we can do is accept the promise by faith, and exclaim, "Thank God!"

"Without the conviction that Christ had conquered death, not for Himself alone, but for all who found life in Him, there would have been no Christianity," says Robert D. Bulkley. "All else was dependent upon this one central fact, that Christ was risen and that we, too, shall rise." We can claim the reality of Christ's resurrection, for it "has entered more deeply than any other historic event into the lives of millions since those early days. It gave the martyrs courage as they faced the perils of the amphitheater."—F. Townley Lord, *The Conquest of Death,* page 73. The early church read the Gospel of John and each member cherished the Saviour's words: "I am come that they might have life, and that they might have it more abundantly." John 10:10. This is the summing up of the purpose of Christ's first advent, and the ever-present hope of the church.

Our attitude toward death and the future life shapes our ideas concerning the purpose of our present existence. "If one then puts aside the existence of God and the possibility of survival as too doubtful to have any effect on one's behavior," says Somerset Maugham, "one has to make up one's mind what is the meaning and use of life. If death ends all, if I have neither to hope for good to come nor to fear evil, I must ask myself what I am here for, and how in these circumstances I must conduct myself."

The Universal Summons

Of the billions of human beings who have lived, worked, loved, and suffered on this earth, only two have escaped from it alive—Enoch and Elijah, who were translated to heaven. Every other being, including the Son of God, has tasted the bitter cup of death.

One man came back to live on this earth after he died and had been buried for four days; but when he returned he gave no account of any life beyond the grave, and he brought no message from the spirit world. That man was Lazarus, a friend of Jesus Christ. On one occasion Lazarus became ill, and before his friend Jesus arrived from a distant part of the country, the man was dead. As Christ and His disciples journeyed toward Bethany, the Saviour broke the sad news of

Lazarus's death. He said, "Our friend Lazarus sleepeth; but I go, that I may awake him out of sleep." And when the disciples were slow to comprehend, Jesus added, "Lazarus is dead." John 11:11, 14.

God's word plainly declares that the dead are asleep. In the day that a man dies his thoughts perish. Psalm 146:4. None of the mental faculties continue in death, for "the dead know not anything." Ecclesiastes 9:5. Each human being is given life, a time when he can decide to be noble, pure, and obedient to God or selfish, proud, and evil. In a world of sin such as ours, men cannot go on living forever. Evil would grow to mammoth proportions if human beings lived for centuries. Therefore a just God allows man to make his decision, to choose his course of action, and then comes the sleep of death. All human beings are left in this unconscious sleep, their life record kept by a merciful Father until the day of judgment and the resurrection.

A loving God shields the dead from the evil, strife, and bloodshed of a world of sin. Comforting is the promise: "He giveth His beloved sleep." Psalm 127:2. It is a rest from the labors and trials, the sorrows and disappointments, of this existence. Hamlet feared that in the "sleep of death dreams may come." But, no; there is nothing to fear, for in quietness and peace the dead rest until they hear the mighty voice of the Son of God.

They Shall Hear His Voice

"The hour is coming," said Jesus, "in the which all that are in the graves shall hear His voice, and shall come forth; they that have done good, unto the resurrection of life; and they that have done evil, unto the resurrection of damnation." John 5:28, 29. There are two distinct resurrections according to this text; the first, to restore the good to life, and the second, to call forth those who have persisted in evil.

The day of triumph over death for the saints who sleep will be when Jesus returns. Paul describes the event in these words: "For the Lord Himself shall descend from heaven with a shout, with the voice of the Archangel, and with the trump of God: and the dead in Christ shall rise first." 1 Thessalonians 4:16.

This is the "lively hope" that Peter speaks of in his first epistle where he emphasizes the promise of eternal life because Jesus was resurrected. The word "lively" means *living* or *full of life*. Truly, Christians have no dead creed; they have a living message: the Pioneer of Life reigns, and He is coming to give eternal life to His faithful ones.

For those who sleep, it will seem but a moment from the hour of their death until they hear the voice of the Son of God. They are unconscious of the passing of time. But suddenly the silence of the grave is broken by a shout of triumph, and the sleeping ones hear His voice! "The hour is coming," said Jesus, "and now is, when the dead shall hear the voice of the Son of God: and they that hear shall live." John 5:25. How fitting it is that those who have obeyed the teachings of Jesus and followed His commandments in this life shall hear Him at the first moment of their resurrection! It is the omnipotent voice of death's Conqueror, the One who, since the day of His release from the tomb, has held the power of death in His hands. When He comes, "then shall be brought to pass the saying that is written, Death is swallowed up in victory." 1 Corinthians 15:54.

We are interested in the exposition of the recently published Protestant commentary, *The Interpreter's Bible,* where a discussion of Paul's teachings on the resurrection is clearly set forth. John Short states, "Christian doctrine is not one of immortality but of resurrection. We shall do well to get this point clear. As expounded by the apostle Paul, whom we believe to have entered more deeply into the mind and spirit of his Lord than any other, man's hope of survival depends not on the inherent immortality of his soul, but on the act of God. ... There is nothing in Paul's writings nor in the New Testament to suggest that the soul is inherently immortal."—Vol. 10, p. 253.

The Gift of Immortality

The transformation from death to life is described in the Scriptures: "For the trumpet will sound, and the dead will be raised imperishable, and we shall be changed. For this perishable nature must put on the imperishable, and this mortal nature must put on immortality." 1 Corinthians 15:52, 53, R.S.V. The change of our bodies from disease and death to purity and immortality will be made at that moment. No man has earned it, for it is "the gift of God."

Our only knowledge concerning the form of the body after it has been invested with eternal life is drawn from the appearance of Jesus after His resurrection. The Gospel narratives reveal that our Lord retained His personality and His form so that He was recognized by the disciples. To doubting Thomas, Jesus showed His nail-pierced hands and His side which had been torn by the soldier's spear. John 20:27. Jesus ate food with His disciples. John 21:12, 13. There was, however, a power in the glorified body which was not confined to time and space. We are told that the resurrected Lord appeared in the room with His disciples when the door was shut. John 20:26. Again He vanished from the sight of two disciples after He had talked with them at the dinner table. Luke 24:31.

"The resurrection of Jesus was a type of the final resurrection of all who sleep in Him. The countenance of the risen Saviour, His manner, His speech, were all familiar to His disciples. As Jesus arose from the dead, so those who sleep in Him are to rise again."—*The Desire of Ages,* page 804.

He Holds the Keys

There is One who possesses the keys to the door of death. Jesus says, "I am He that liveth, and was dead; and, behold, I am alive for evermore, Amen; and have the keys of hell and of death." Revelation 1:18. To possess "the keys of hell and of death" is the symbol of the authority of the Son of God over these enemies of man. Jesus gained full control over hell and death by His victory over sin and Satan. When the King of kings comes in glory, these enemies shall be destroyed. 1 Corinthians 15:26.

Thank God, the keys are in His hands! No spirit medium can tamper with the dead. No earthly hand can desecrate the life or character of those who are now sleeping. Only the Son of God can take the keys and open the door. He alone can call the sleeping ones from their rest.

We sorrow not as those who have no hope, for Jesus is our assurance of resurrection and life. "Wherefore comfort one another with these words," says Paul. 1 Thessalonians 4:18. Death shall be forever wiped from the universe. "There can be no doubt that in the eyes of the apostle, and surely for the people to whom he wrote, death was a fearful calamity; it is an evening that threatens with oblivion all that we hold dear. How can it appear otherwise? What could give greater cause for rejoicing than the assurance, vindicated and justified by a resurrection which could only be ascribed to a God of righteousness and love and power, that death would finally be utterly vanquished?"—*The Interpreter's Bible,* vol. 10, pp. 249, 250.

Sometime ago I was driving in New Orleans in the vicinity of the cemeteries. I turned into one street that led to an iron fence—the boundary of the graveyard. My eye caught sight of a sign on a nearby telephone pole. It read: "Dead End." It seemed to symbolize the hopelessness of death for those who have not found the Life-giver.

The Christian belief in eternal life is a sacred trust that is not to be treated lightly. We believe that our talents and time are entrusted to us so that we will make the most of them. The child of God is not building merely for threescore years and ten. He is building both for time and for eternity. Yes, what we think about life, what we think about ourselves, and what we think about God, are all dependent upon our belief in the future—eternal life with our Redeemer and our God.

Let us give thanks that we live this side of the resurrection of our Lord. We can see down the highway of life, and it holds no "dead end" for us. The Pioneer of Life went before us and blazed the way to heaven. He calls to His trusting children, "Follow Me. . . . I am the way." With gratitude we can say, "Thanks be to God, who gives us the victory through our Lord Jesus Christ." 1 Corinthians 15:57, R.S.V.

FACING OUR SORROW

~9~

Strength to Endure

A WONDERFUL stained-glass window once adorned a famous cathedral in Southern Europe. Pilgrims from distant lands journeyed to the spot to gaze upon the masterpiece of art. One day a violent windstorm struck with such force it sent the window crashing to the marble floor, shattering it into hundreds of pieces. The caretakers gathered up the fragments, put them in a box, and stored them in the basement. Months passed and on a certain day a stranger came to town and inquired about the famous window. When told of its fate, he desired to see the fragments. When shown the box of shattered glass, the stranger asked, "Would you give these to me?"

"Take them along," said the caretaker; "they are no longer of value to the cathedral."

After many months had passed an invitation came to the custodians of the cathedral, asking them to visit the studio of a famous artist in a distant city. At the appointed hour the men arrived, and the artist ushered them into a room hung with a large canvas. When the curtain was dropped, the custodians saw a stained-glass window surpassing the beauty of the lost

(73)

masterpiece. As the visitors gazed in wonder, the artist said, "This window was created from the fragments of the shattered one in your cathedral. I return the broken pieces to you in the form of this picture. It is now ready to be transported to your church."

For many of us the pattern of life has been shattered by sorrow or tragedy. Broken pieces lie about us, and we feel as Job did when he said, "Wherefore is light given to him that is in misery, and life unto the bitter in soul?" Job 3:20. The complaint is a common one, for the despondent person frequently asks, "Why was I born?" But these moods will pass, especially when one's faith is anchored to the Rock of Ages. Out of the ruins of today can rise hope and happiness tomorrow.

"The longing for the rest of the grave is the mood of intense weariness and disease; and it is counteracted by the mood of restored health, which longs for activity, even in heaven."— *The Pulpit Commentary,* Job, page 60. When the heart is sad, the physical health is affected. Job said, "My eye has grown dim from grief, and all my members are like a shadow." Job 17:7, R.S.V.

To brood over one's disappointment, bereavement, or illness only clouds the mind and weakens the body. "It is a positive duty to resist melancholy, discontented thoughts and feelings,—as much a duty as it is to pray." "Let the burden of your own weakness and sorrow and pain be cast upon the compassionate Saviour."—*The Ministry of Healing,* pages 251, 257.

Concerning those who are burdened with pain or who have brought trouble to others, the apostle Paul wrote the Christians: "So you should rather turn to forgive and comfort him, or he may be overwhelmed by excessive sorrow." 2 Corinthians

2:7, R.S.V. Men and women need the helping hand of one who has received courage and strength from God. A word spoken at the right moment may lift a discouraged soul from despair and set his feet on the road to new horizons.

When Mary Coburn lived in a New York apartment she practiced her vocal lessons faithfully every day, not realizing what the influence of her singing might bring. In *The Reader's Digest* she recounts her experience as she was at a discouraging point in her career. "Almost panicky, I grabbed at a piece of music. It was Albert Hay Malotte's beautiful setting of 'The Lord's Prayer.' My courage returned. Jubilantly I stood in the middle of the room and sang it with a full heart. I must have sung it five or six times.

"Several days later I heard a rustle at my door, and turned to see a note being slipped under it. It read: 'Dear Neighbor: If ever you feel discouraged, perhaps this will hearten you. Things have been going badly for me—so badly I didn't want to live any longer. When I'd hear you practicing I'd snap out of it a little, because you sounded as though you had something to live for. Finally the other night I decided to end my life. I went into the kitchen and turned on the gas. Then I heard you singing. It was 'The Lord's Prayer.' Suddenly I realized what I was doing. I turned off the gas, opened the windows and drank in the fresh air. You sang that song several times. Well—you saved my life. You gave me the courage to make a decision I should have made long ago. Now life is all I could hope it to be. Thanks always.' "

There is a prescription for spiritual morale in the thirty-seventh psalm that never fails if it is diligently followed. The fifth verse is particularly apropos, for we read, "Commit thy way unto the Lord; trust also in Him; and He shall bring it to pass." Our heavenly Father is a mender of broken hearts.

Trust Him, and He will take the fragments that have been scattered by sin and sorrow and create a new life that will shine as the stars forever in His eternal kingdom.

Only One Answer

For the ordeal of death and tears such as our world faces today there is only one answer—faith in the risen Christ and in His word. The hope of the resurrection takes away hopeless grief, for the Christian does "not grieve as others do who have no hope." 1 Thessalonians 4:13, R.S.V. Because we have suffered a stunning blow does not mean that we can sit down and quit. We face the dawn of each day with a God who loves us. "If we are called upon to meet bereavement, let us accept the bitter cup, remembering that a Father's hand holds it to our lips."—*The Ministry of Healing,* page 233.

Our heavenly Father does not want to see our lives ruined by sorrow and mourning. There is service to render to others; blessings to pass on to those in greater need. Let us accept the lesson and look up into the face of our loving Saviour. "Suffering is the emery wheel upon which the cutting edge of Christian character is sharpened. It is by our patience, patience under trial, that we are to 'win our souls.' For this reason we may 'triumph even in our troubles,' knowing that out of these is born endurance, character, and hope. 'The pain God is allowed to guide' ends in repentance and new character."— F. Olin Stockwell, in *The Christian Century,* Feb. 11, 1953.

In the farewell words of Moses to the children of Israel is the sublime promise:

> "The eternal God is your dwelling place,
> and underneath are the everlasting arms."
> Deuteronomy 33:27, R.S.V.

The figure is that of a parent supporting a child who is attempting to walk. How well Moses knew the strength of God's "everlasting arms." The door had been closed on his hopes, and he was forced to renounce his dearest plans. Like Moses, let us take courage, for God is by us in the shadows. "Always underneath and round about are His everlasting arms. We never make our way alone through the world. Faces may change and conditions may alter, but God is the same yesterday, today, and forever."—*The Interpreter's Bible,* vol. 2, p. 556.

The Son of God trusted His Father, and He was willing to accept the bitter with the sweet in His earthly ministry. When we read the terrible story of Christ's death on the cross, we may feel that He was the victim of powers beyond His control. This is not true, for the Saviour suffered only because He *willed to suffer.* To His disciples He said: "For this reason the Father loves Me, because I lay down My life, that I may take it again. No one takes it from Me, but I lay it down of My own accord." John 10:17, 18, R.S.V. The ideal the Saviour set before us is perfect obedience to God's will. Jesus exemplified His submission to His Father when He said to Peter, "Shall I not drink the cup which the Father has given Me?"

As the potter takes the clay, wets it, and kneads it until it is pliable, so the Master Potter works upon our lives. When the clay is moist enough and perfectly pliable, the potter shapes it into a beautiful and useful vessel. In the same manner the Master of men molds and fashions us if we submit to His will. The trials, afflictions, and heartaches that seem cruel and to no purpose may be the essential experience to develop sympathy, patience, and love in the heart.

Can we not look back over some of the earlier experiences in our life and see how divine Providence was leading us when the way seemed mysterious and dark? Shall we not take heart when we are faced with perplexing moments today? Shall we not be submissive and teachable, learning that even the deepest tragedy does not come by chance?

Dr. Norman Vincent Peale recounts the experience of a skiing party in the Canadian Rockies who came to a dangerous transverse valley where avalanches threatened to destroy them. The guide told the group not to call, whistle, or talk in loud tones, for it might start the slide of death. In the party was a girl in her twenties who realized the danger. She began to whimper and cry, and said, "I can't do it. I'm terrified. I simply can't do it."

The leader of the party looked at the hysterical girl and said quietly, "The Lord has watched over you throughout you life hasn't He? You believe that, don't you?"

"Yes," sobbed the girl.

"Well, then can't you trust Him to take care of you for the next twenty minutes?" asked the leader.

The frightened girl came through the ordeal triumphantly, for she remembered how God had stood by her side through every experience.

In referring to the overwhelming disaster He faced, Jesus asked His disciples: " 'Are you able to drink the cup that I drink, or to be baptized with the baptism with which I am baptized?' And they said to Him, 'We are able' " Mark 10:38, 39, R.S.V., James and John were sincere in thinking they were able to drink from the cup of suffering and to receive the baptism of trial; but when the test came, "they all forsook Him, and fled." The disciples dreamed of doing great deeds for their Lord if He were a king; but they melted away from His side when a mob came with staves and sticks to take their Leader off to court. They could not face scorn, ridicule, and the jeers of the crowd. In like manner we might be ready to lay down our lives in heroic conquests for the cross, but we give up when petty trials, hardships, or light persecution come our way.

Courage to Carry On

There is an impressive lesson in seeing it through with God in the life of the prophet Ezekiel. Tragic loss came to him, for he wrote, "At even my wife died; and I did in the morning as I was commanded." Ezekiel 24:18. It was not that the man of God was insensible to his loss, for he said the light of his home went out and the desire of his heart had passed away; but he had spiritual stamina and a true perspective of life so that he could go on with his daily duties, even though his heart was broken.

A Christian woman who had lost her husband continued to mourn for weeks and months. Finally her little son came to her one day and asked, "Mother, is God dead?"

"No, dear," the woman replied; "but your father is."

The child's question challenged the woman's mind, however, and she put aside her grief and accepted life's responsibilities, knowing that her God still lived.

Our worth to our fellow men is measured, not by what we begin, but by what we complete. To carry on in the face of tragedy, to work in the face of failure, to pray in the face of defeat, to smile courageously through our tears—these come only as we have faith to look up and say, "Dear God, Thy will, not mine, be done."

To those who are in sorrow there are special words direct from the loving Saviour: "Blessed are they that mourn: for they shall be comforted." Matthew 5:4. The Greek word for *comfort* may be translated "to call to the side of." The English word *comfort* comes from the Latin root which has the idea of strength: *con-fortis,* or to endure with fortitude. God's comfort to the sorrowing is no anesthetic; it is a tender, reinforcing strength, when Christ comes to the side of the sufferer and enables him to go forward triumphant.

> "The Lord is near to the brokenhearted,
> and saves the crushed in spirit."
> Psalm 34:18, R.S.V.

Someday We'll Understand

The mirrors of the apostle Paul's day were made of polished metal, and the city of Corinth was famous for those made of silver or brass. However, they were not perfect reflectors, and since they were not they became an object lesson to the apostle of man's imperfect knowledge in this life. Writing to the church at Corinth, the apostle declared, "For now we see in a mirror dimly, but then face to face. Now I know in part; then I shall understand fully, even as I have been fully understood." 1 Corinthians 13:12, R.S.V. Moffatt translates the phrase, "the baffling reflections in a mirror."

Yes, often the reflections in the mirror of life are dim and baffling. Our faith is scarcely strong enough to see God. Yet we can be thankful for the dim reflection, since it is the promise that someday we shall see Him face to face!

Paul felt his physical resources ebbing away as he gave himself wholly to the preaching of the gospel. Tired and sometimes discouraged, yet he could say, "So we do not lose heart. Though our outer nature is wasting away, our inner nature is being renewed every day. For this slight momentary affliction is preparing for us an eternal weight of glory beyond all comparison." 2 Corinthians 4:16, 17, R.S.V.

"*Affliction* here is transmuted into glory beyond. . . . The affliction is *slight* and *momentary* by comparison with the *glory* which is massive and unfading. . . . Our judgment of things depends on the background against which we see them, as the background of a picture gives us perspective and qualifies the foreground. . . . If we have no belief in God or a future life, if we know nothing of Christ, if our view of the world is that it is merely a mechanical process without spiritual value or purpose, everything will be colored by this outlook. Trouble will be a disaster; pain will be a calamity; and sorrow a tragedy. But if we have the Christian view, the sufferings of earth will be no more than the chisel strokes of the Sculptor, forgotten in the beauty of the statue which He is shaping from the marble, or even welcomed as the means of His achievement."—*The Interpreter's Bible,* vol. 10, pp. 323, 324.

The mind can but faintly imagine the wonders of the earth restored to perfect beauty as God shall present it to those who love Him. Through our tears and blinding sorrow we hear the promise: "Eye hath not seen, nor ear heard, neither have entered into the heart of man, the things which God hath prepared for them that love Him." 1 Corinthians 2:9.

We will never be homesick for this better world, however, until we are dissatisfied with this one. Ellen G. White states, "We need to keep ever before us this vision of things unseen. It is thus that we shall be able to set a right value on the things of eternity and the things of time. It is this that will give us power to influence others for the higher life."—*The Ministry of Healing,* page 508.

TO KNOW GOD'S WILL

~10~

The Test of Discipleship

A WEALTHY manufacturer went to one of the ablest architects in America and asked him to prepare plans for a new factory to cost ten million dollars. The architect set to work studying and analyzing the requirements, the site of the building, and the necessary materials. Finally he completed the blueprints for the huge plant—a masterpiece of architectural engineering. When the manufacturer received the plans he studied them carefully, but soon he cast them aside and ordered carpenters, steelworkers, and bricklayers to work on a building he had crudely sketched. The structure was a hodgepodge of slovenly, poorly planned construction, inadequate for the needs of the company.

You say, "No smart businessman would be so stupid as to build such a structure."

Perhaps not, but this is a parable of what millions of human beings are doing with the temple of their lives. God has a perfect plan for each of us if we submit to His will. We can follow the divine blueprint or we can put it aside for our selfish, inadequate, poorly conceived ideas and attitudes. The choice is ours.

Those who are determined to have their own way follow

a stubborn course that ends in disaster. The wise man wrote, "There is a way which seemeth right unto a man, but the end thereof are the ways of death." Proverbs 14:12. When we persist in demanding our own way we are actually fighting against God. "Whenever men choose their own way, they place themselves in controversy with God. They will have no place in the kingdom of heaven, for they are at war with the very principles of heaven."—*Thoughts From the Mount of Blessing,* pages 82, 83.

Headstrong and rebellious, man does not want to obey or to submit to God's will. The heavenly Father is longing to teach us how to find happiness here and in the hereafter, but we lack faith and confidence in Him. It is essential, in these days of ruined dreams and perished hopes, to get back to the simple faith expressed by Isaiah:

> "Behold, God is my salvation;
>   I will trust, and will not be afraid;
>   for the Lord God is my strength and my song,
>   and He has become my salvation."
>   Isaiah 12:2, R.S.V.

The secret of victorious Christian living resides in the trusting heart. Warren Seabury, a missionary to China, wrote, "I do not know what is before me, but I am building my nest in the greatness of God." This confidence is supported by a knowledge of the Eternal One. We are instructed through His word and by the impressions that come to our minds by the Holy Spirit. Isaiah declared, "Though the Lord give you the bread of adversity and the water of affliction, yet your Teacher will not hid Himself any more, but your eyes shall see your Teacher. And your ears shall hear a word behind you, saying, 'This is the way, walk in

it,' when you turn to the right or when you turn to the left."
Isaiah 30:20, 21, R.S.V.

God speaks to man in various ways so that all may hear His
voice if they will only listen. Through His creative works He
communicates to us, for, as Paul states, "Ever since the creation
of the world His invisible nature, namely, His eternal power
and Deity, has been clearly perceived in the things that have
been made." Romans 1:20, R.S.V. Sin has marred the Creator's
handiwork, and the evolution theory robs God of His rightful
place in nature, yet to the discerning mind the universe is a
sublime expression of God's character.

The Eternal One speaks to humanity through His Son, the
Word "made flesh." Jesus Christ came to teach men and
women the eternal truths concerning salvation and to demon-
strate how much the Father loved His children. "We know
that the Son of God is come, and hath given us an understanding, that we may know Him that is true." 1 John 5:20.

God communicates to us through chosen human beings. He
spoke "in time past unto the fathers by the prophets." Hebrews
1:1. These truths have been brought together in Holy Scripture
and become a guidebook for the Christian. As we delve into
the blessed Book, the wisdom and love of God in the plan of
redemption is revealed to us.

A Willingness to Accept God's Will

God speaks to man through the Holy Spirit. The conscience,
when subject to the divine will, is guided into the way of
truth. To His disciples Jesus made the promise that the Comforter would "teach you all things, and bring all things to your
remembrance, whatsoever I have said unto you." John 14:26.

With every prayer that we offer there must be a willingness
to accept God's answer. If we have the spirit of Jesus we will

pray as He did: "Thy will be done." The Scriptures are a defense against the foes that assail us. Doubt, discouragement, and despair are the enemy's instruments to destroy faith, but we have a tested and true weapon, "the sword of the Spirit, which is the word of God." Ephesians 6:17.

The man or woman who knows God's word and treasures it in his heart "shall not be afraid of evil tidings: his heart is fixed, trusting in the Lord." Paul desired every follower of Christ to be filled with "the knowledge of His will." Colossians 1:9. Suffering becomes more understandable as we accept God's blueprint for us.

"God reveals His will to us in His word, the Holy Scriptures. His voice is also revealed in His providential workings; and it will be recognized if we do not separate our souls from Him by walking in our own ways, doing according to our own wills, and following the promptings of an unsanctified heart, until the senses have become so confused that eternal things are not discerned, and the voice of Satan is so disguised that it is accepted as the voice of God."—*Messages to Young People,* page 156.

If we have not heard the voice of God saying, "This is the way, walk in it," it is because we have not trained ourselves to listen. It is possible for us to become so busy running here and there on God's service we never actually know what He wants us to do. Jesus warned His followers of such a tragic plight when He said, "Not everyone that saith unto Me, Lord, Lord, shall enter into the kingdom of heaven; but he that doeth the will of My Father which is in heaven." Matthew 7:21.

Obedience to God's commands is the acid test of discipleship. If we were left to follow our own whims and desires, we would lose our way. Therefore we are asked to accept God's will and keep His commandments. The motivation for our obedience must come from the heart, that is, the will, or it is worthless. The apostle Paul admonishes us to do "the will of God from the heart." Ephesians 6:6.

It is breath-taking to realize what can happen as we love Jesus Christ and obey His words. Here is the staggering promise: "If a man loves Me, he will keep My word, and My Father will love him, and We will come to him and make Our home with him." John 14:23, R.S.V. Yes, our heart can be God's home. It is a poor place we have to offer Him, not worthy of His entrance; yet He says He will come in and make it His *home!* Dwight L. Moody describes the effect of the abiding presence of our Lord in these words: "There are two lives for the Christian, one for the world, and one with God. If you dwell constantly at the feet of Jesus, it will save you many a painful hour."

God's negative answers sometimes carry with them His richest gifts. John Ellis Large, in *Think on These Things,* tells the well-known parable of the three trees that grew in the forest long ago: "The first tree prayed that, when it was hewn down, it might become part of the timbers of a noble palace, the most magnificent building ever shaped by the creative hands of men. . . . Instead, it was faced with the bitter fact that its lovely grain was being used to throw a rude stable together. But it was the stable in which the Christ Child was born!

"The second tree petitioned God that, when the ax should be laid to its roots, its planks might be fashioned into the hull of the lordliest vessel that ever sailed the seven seas. . . . Instead, when it was chopped down, it was used to form the hull of a lowly fishing vessel; and the tree resented the insult to its grandeur. But that insignificant schooner was the one from which Jesus preached His incomparable words at the edge of the little Sea of Galilee!

"The third tree beseeched God that it might *never* feel the bite of the cruel ax, but that it might go on for years pointing its proud finger toward the sky. . . . Instead, the dark day came when the woodsmen arrived and laid the sharp blade to its resisting roots; and it cried out against God with every blow. But the shaken tree was fated to become the crossarms and the upright of the cross of Calvary, destined to point its noble finger toward the sky forever!

"Not a single one of those trees lived to see its fondest wish come true. Not a single one got its deepest prayer answered, nor its own will fulfilled. But God, in fulfilling His will for those three trees, granted them a fulfillment infinitely beyond anything they could have desired or hoped for!"

To Do His Will

When Jesus struggled through the dark hours in the Garden of Gethsemane, He longed to be saved from crucifixion and death. Therefore He prayed, "O My Father, if it be possible, let this cup pass from Me: nevertheless not as I will, but as Thou wilt." Matthew 26:39. Three times Jesus uttered this petition. He might have rebelled against drinking the cup of sorrow, but He was submissive to the will of His Father. He turned His eyes once more toward heaven and breathed a prayer of submission to the divine will. "If this cup may not pass away from Me, except I drink it, Thy will be done." Verse 42. It was in Gethsemane that the Son of God prayed through to victory. He was triumphant in the hour of deepest trial and suffering! When the soldiers came into the garden to take Jesus, Peter was ready to fight; but the Saviour answered, "Put up thy sword into the sheath: the cup which My Father hath given Me, shall I not drink it?" John 18:11. Prayer had prepared the Master for the suffering before Him.

"The obedience that Christ rendered, God requires from human beings today. He served His Father with love, in willingness and freedom."—*Christ's Object Lessons,* page 282. At the foot of the Mount of Olives there is even today a spot among the gray-leaved olive trees called Gethsemane. It has become a shrine because here Jesus was willing to place everything in His Father's hands. This was where He trusted to the limit.

No wonder Paul declares that Jesus "became obedient unto death, even the death of the cross." Philippians 2:8. And the writer of the book of Hebrews emphasizes that Christ learned "obedience by the things which He suffered." Hebrews 5:8. The prayers of our Lord in Gethsemane are the key to all victorious Christian living, for they mean unconditional surrender. "When a man is in tune with Christ," says E. H. Pruden, "his lips will be saying and his hands will be doing what Christ wants."

We cannot answer all the questions concerning life and death, good and evil; but these become insignificant if only we have confidence in the eternal goodness of the Almighty. The history of much that has been called Christianity has often been a chronicle of distrust and fear; but when we say, as did Isaiah, "I will trust, and not be afraid," we will triumph gloriously. The end will ultimately explain and vindicate that which is darkness today. The experiences of life may be hard and harrowing, inscrutable and irreconcilable, but they are fertile soil in which the finest sort of faith can grow.

In a castle on the Rhine River once lived a baron who had grown bitter because of the hypocrisy of his supposed friends. To help pass the time in his rock-bound fortress he hung wires from one point to another to make an aeolian harp on which the winds might play. Days and nights came and winds blew, yet there was no music from the huge harp. The baron interpreted all of this to be a sign of God's displeasure. One evening, however, the sky was filled with storm clouds and a fierce tempest came with the darkness. As the lonely baron paced his halls, he suddenly heard it! The wild air was filled with music. His harp was singing with joy and passion above the roar of the storm. Then it was the baron knew the truth. The thick heavy wires could give out music only in a time of storm and tempestuous winds.

So it may be with our spiritual experience. The darkness falls, and hurricanes of doubt and suffering blow—and in those hours we discover the sweetest music of divine love.

> Our sweetest songs are those that tell
> of saddest thought.
> —Percy B. Shelley.

The soul that is sure of God and rests upon His will accepts the whole scheme of pain and trial. The more such a faith is tried, the deeper it will hide itself in God. "Therefore," says the apostle Peter, "let those who suffer according to God's will do right and entrust their souls to a faithful Creator." 1 Peter 4:19, R.S.V.

An anonymous Confederate soldier wrote this touching meditation in time of battle:

"I asked God for strength, that I might achieve—I was made weak, that I might learn humbly to obey. . . .

"I asked for help that I might do greater things—I was given infirmity, that I might do better things. . . .

"I asked for riches, that I might be happy—I was given poverty, that I might be wise. . . .

"I asked for power, that I might have the praise of men—I was given weakness, that I might feel the need of God. . . .

"I asked for all things, that I might enjoy life—I was given life, that I might enjoy all things. . . .

"I got nothing that I asked for—but everything I had hoped for. . . .

"Almost despite myself, my unspoken prayers were answered. I am, among all men, most richly blessed!"

Our Father has not minimized the trial and suffering we shall have to face. He tells us we will go through tribulations and trials, but He also promises to help us triumph over the worst of them. The beloved John heard the words of commendation that will be spoken to those who are victorious in the final conflict. Of these valiant sons of God the apostle wrote, "These are they which came out of great tribulation, and have washed their robes, and made them white in the blood of the Lamb." Revelation 7:14. Upon the sea of glass the conquerors will gather. They will have "gotten the victory" and will be able to sing a new song before the throne of God.

"When the earthly warfare is accomplished, and the saints are all gathered home, our first theme will be the song of Moses, the servant of God. The second theme will be the song of the Lamb, the song of grace and redemption. . . . This is the theme, this is the song,—Christ all and in all,—in anthems of praise resounding through heaven from thousands and ten thousand times ten thousand and an innumerable company of the redeemed host. All unite in this song of Moses and of the Lamb. It is a new song, for it was never before sung in heaven." —*Testimonies to Ministers,* page 433.

These soldiers of the cross have learned discipline; they know how to obey. They have kept the commandments of God and have held firm in the faith of Jesus. It is of this hour that John was thinking when he wrote, "He that doeth the will of God abideth forever." 1 John 2:17.

Patient obedience will characterize Christ's remnant people. They will obey God's law, honor Him as the Creator, and remember His Sabbath. In the remnant group will be found no hypocrisy, for no guile is in their mouths. They will follow the example of their Lord as He prayed, "Thy will be done."

The victors will possess "the faith of Jesus." It is a faith that looks beyond the wickedness, the depravity, the moral bankruptcy, and the spiritual disillusionment of a lost civilization to the light that shines brighter unto the perfect day. It is a faith founded upon the word of God, for every Christian will be able to answer, "It is written." It is a faith that surrenders to the Eternal One and says, "Take me as I am and mold my will to Thy pattern that I may be Your child forever."

COMFORTING THOSE WHO MOURN

~⦾‖⦿~

Hope for the Hopeless

THERE is no home on earth but will have its hush," says an old Spanish proverb, describing the universal effect of sorrow. Yet no matter what our loss may be, we still have a duty to perform in life. Even though we may have sustained a stunning blow, we cannot sit down and quit. To carry on in the face of tragedy, to work in the face of defeat, to smile courageously through our tears—all these take faith in God and in His promises.

There is no more depressing experience for a minister than to be called to conduct the funeral of a loved one in a family that has no faith in God. The finality of the loss, the unrestrained agony, the bewildering bitterness, are beyond description. Paul told the Christian believers that they were not to sorrow "as others which have no hope." 1 Thessalonians 4:13. And to the hopeless and despairing we are to offer a genuine hope—Jesus Christ, "the resurrection, and the life."

The Saviour knew the lonely agony and despair that humanity experiences. In the prophetic words of Psalm 69:20 we see the suffering of the Messiah: "Reproach hath broken My heart; and I am full of heaviness: and I looked for some to take pity, but there was none; and for comforters, but I found none."

It is a source of strength to know that Jesus went through the deepest torrents of suffering without faltering, and as the result He is able to comfort the afflicted and brokenhearted.

The original Greek word for "sympathy" means "to suffer with" another person. Thus, when Jesus sympathizes with us He suffers with us in all our afflictions. The pain-wracked world needs Christians who "suffer with" their brother man. This experience comes only as we feel a kinship and a oneness with those who mourn. The prophet Ezekiel learned how to be tolerant and sympathetic when he visited the captives who lived by the Chebar River. He says, "I sat where they sat, and remained there astonished among them seven days." Ezekiel 3:15. As the prophet looked through the eyes of these people he became sensitive to their pathetic condition, and their need "overwhelmed" him. (R.S.V.)

We would be shocked out of our smugness and lethargy if we would leave our more sheltered existence and mingle for a time with the downtrodden, the outcast, the helpless, and the underprivileged. "Unless a helping hand is held out to them, they will sink lower and lower."—*The Ministry of Healing,* page 172. As ambassadors for Christ, we must minister to every class of people.

When we follow in the footsteps of the Master we will "rejoice with them that do rejoice, and weep with them that weep." Romans 12:15. Let us never forget that "there are multitudes struggling with poverty, compelled to labor hard for small wages, and able to secure but the barest necessities of life. Toil and deprivation, with no hope of better things, make their burden very heavy. When pain and sickness are added, the burden is almost insupportable. Careworn and oppressed, they know not where to turn for relief. Sympathize with them in their trials, their heartaches, and disappointments. This will open

the way for you to help them. Speak to them of God's promises, pray with and for them, inspire them with hope."—*The
Ministry of Healing,* page 158.

Helping Those Who Mourn

How shall we help a person in his hour of grief? We long
to do something to ease his pain and suffering, but we feel
incompetent and we are afraid we will do the wrong thing.
Howard Whitman recently gathered the suggestions of clergy-
men who had much experience in helping the bereaved, and he
sets forth the salient points in an excellent article in *The Christian Advocate.*

We should not attempt to minimize the grief of the individual or try to divert him from his sorrow when it is fresh and
acute. Let the sorrowing one talk of his loss. It is often a good
thing to recount the life of the loved one who is gone. The one
who mourns should face the reality of the loss, accept the fact of
death, and go forward with God's help in a new and altered life.

To the sorrowing we can be good listeners. If they wish to
empty themselves of pent-up sorrow, let them do it, for grief
cannot long be harbored or cherished in the bosom without
damaging the outlook on life. Let us listen thoughtfully, and
when we do speak we will be ready to reassure the sorrowing
one that God loves him.

Do not allow your sympathy and interest in the sorrowing
one to be a thing of a moment. He may need help most acutely
after the lonely days have lengthened into months. Whitman
wisely suggests: "Keep in touch. See your friend more often
than you did before. See him for any purpose—for lunch together, for a drive in the country, for shopping, for an evening
visit. He has suffered a deep loss. Your job is to show him, by
implication, how much he still has left. Your being with him

is proof to him that he still has resources to draw upon."

We can show our love by little acts of kindness, helping lift the petty details until grief is assuaged. We can help the sorrowing get out of the vacuum by showing them how they are needed by others and how they can help the community and the church. Tennyson well said, "I must lose myself in action, lest I wither in despair."

The heart may be numb and the home desolate, but the mood of despair can be overcome. Let love find its way into the heart of the grief-stricken—love for the needy and love for those less fortunate. The authors of *When Sorrow Comes,* Grace Perkins Oursler and April Armstrong, give this prescription: "Fill the hours overbrimming, fill other hearts with the life-giving love you have lost. Don't let the wellspring of love dry up from lack of use. You have lost one outlet for those springs of human affection. Remember we were born to love and to give."—Page 88.

The Example of Jesus

As Jesus walked along the country roads or on the narrow streets of the cities of Palestine, He felt compassion for every person He met. "The word translated compassion is actually a much stronger word: it implies pain of love. He saw the people of His land as shepherdless people. They were as if wolves had harried them and left them bleeding, because they had none to lead and protect them."—*The Interpreter's Bible,* vol. 7, p. 360.

The "pain of love" caused the Master to pour out His life in service. He taught in the synagogues, He healed the sick, and He fed the hungry. Matthew depicts the sympathizing Saviour in these words: "When He saw the multitudes, He was moved with compassion on them, because they fainted, and were scattered abroad, as sheep having no shepherd." Matthew 9:36.

The Son of God never attended a funeral except to turn it into a time of rejoicing. One day as He was approaching the gate of the city of Nain, He saw a funeral procession for the only son of a widow. As the Saviour stood at the side of the sorrowing mother, His heart was touched with love and pity, and He said, "Weep not." Then He called the dead man back to life. This same Jesus is touched by our grief. To us who mourn, He says, "Weep not. I am the resurrection and the life." His heart has the same unchanging love for heartbroken mothers today that He had that day at Nain.

Our Lord was sorrowful as the time drew near when He must leave His disciples, for He realized they needed help and comfort from heaven. Therefore Jesus said, "I will pray the Father, and He shall give you another Comforter, that He may abide with you forever." John 14:16. "Another Comforter." Yes, Jesus had been the solace, the comfort of His followers, and to all His children through succeeding generations He sends the blessed Comforter, the Holy Spirit.

Pointing the Brokenhearted to Christ

When the church is filled with the power of the Holy Spirit, every member will lift the fallen and help bind up the wounds of the afflicted. While each person is to bear his own burdens as best he can, yet there are times when the load grows too heavy. Then Paul's admonition applies: "Bear ye one another's burdens, and so fulfill the law of Christ." Galatians 6:2. The best way to increase our faith and to strengthen our courage is to share them with others. Life to be happy must be shared; it smothers when it is shut up in itself.

The experience of a woman who had served the church for twenty years is recounted by Oscar F. Blackwelder. This Christian mother came to her pastor and asked, "Do you remember the wretched health I had when you first learned to know me, what a nervous wreck I was?" Then she added, "I have had to bear so many burdens in my family that today I am a relatively well woman." Helping to lift the burdens of her loved ones had made her strong to bear her own.

The peace of the Christian is not an abstract idea or quality; it is a Person. If we would correctly translate Ephesians 2:14 we would find that it is more than "He is our peace." The full meaning is "He is the Author of our peace." When we have learned of the Master and He has written His enduring peace in our hearts, we can point the distressed and sorrowing to Him. The weaker a soul may be, the stronger will be the arm of the Saviour. The heavier the burden that is weighing upon the heart, the greater the lifting power of our Burden Bearer.

In order to dramatize the need of the helpless and sorrowing, Jesus identifies Himself with them, and He asks us to see not their need but *His*. In the parable of the last judgment our Lord described the humble, compassionate Christians who saw the hunger, nakedness, loneliness, and sorrow of the masses, and who did something to help them. To this group came the King's blessing: "Inasmuch as ye have done it unto one of the least of these My brethren, ye have done it unto Me." Matthew 25:40.

These lowly followers of the Master were amazed to learn that they were doing a personal service to their King. They loved their fellow men, they saw a great need, and they acted because the "pain of love" impelled them. In contrast to this group there were the "professed Christians" who would have done anything for Jesus if they could have served Him personally, but they would not stoop to help the poor and the fallen. They had divorced their religion from daily life; it was a theory, not a living, loving experience.

Our Saviour is willing to make humanity's need His own. He goes incognito in the poor, the helpless, the sorrowing. "He identifies Himself as being in person *the very sufferer*. Mark, selfish Christian: every neglect of the needy poor, the orphan, the fatherless, is a neglect of Jesus in their person."—*Testimonies,* vol. 2, p. 26. (Italics ours.)

Qualified to Serve

Alcoholics Anonymous is doing much good in helping release men and women from the throes of alcoholism. The organization is successful because those who have been delivered from the curse work to help those who are victims. Members visit the sick person and tell him how they gained the victory over alcohol. They can say, "I've been over the road and I know you can triumph, too."

In like manner the Christian can help the oppressed and fainthearted, for after he has experienced the comfort of God he can witness to what it has done for him. The comfort is founded upon a close fellowship with the heavenly Father. A missionary was teaching an Indian woman the Lord's Prayer. As he began with the first two words, "Our Father," her eyes lighted and she said, "I do not need to know any more. If God is our Father that changes everything."

Yes, everything is wonderfully changed because our Father comforts us. And "the Father of mercies and God of all comfort, who comforts us in all our affliction" is with us, "so that we may be able to comfort those who are in any affliction, with the comfort with which we ourselves are comforted." 2 Corinthians 1:3, 4, R.S.V. In commenting on this verse, *The Interpreter's Bible* declares, " 'The comfort with which we ourselves are comforted by God' is therefore the only form of comfort which is effective. Sympathy which merely assures people that we feel for them can do little. It may even increase their trouble by communicating a sense of our helplessness. It may feed their self-pity. The true comforter is one who can carry to others the strength of an experience in which God has given him the victory. This comfort is of universal application. It applies to all situations. It speaks to the hearts of people 'in any affliction.' All troubles find healing in a right relationship with God, and in the opening of the mind to His message."—Vol. 10, p. 281.

We never receive peace in wholesale quantities that will last for months or years; it is a daily possession. Thrilling are the words of the apostle Paul to the Christian: "God's peace, that surpasses all our dreams, keep guard over your hearts and minds in Christ Jesus." Philippians 4:7, Moffatt.

With a trusting heart as our precious possession, we can be a powerful influence upon those who are bewildered, helpless, and defeated. Isaiah pictures the mission of the child of God thus:

"The Lord God has given me
   the tongue of those who are taught,
that I may know how to sustain with a word
   him that is weary."

We are taught when we sit at the feet of Jesus. His words will become so much a part of our thinking that we will transmit them to others, and thus men will know we are the Saviour's disciples.

Since "no man is an island, entire of itself; every man is a piece of the continent, a part of the main," we are all bound together by our mutual needs. Intercessory prayer must be a part of the spiritual experience of every sincere Christian. When we pray for a soul in desperate need, we must be ready to go into action as God directs to help answer our petitions.

Jesus prayed for His disciples. To faltering Peter He said, "I have prayed for thee, that thy faith fail not." Luke 22:32. Furthermore, our High Priest "ever liveth to make intercession" for us. Hebrews 7:25. To follow the example of our Lord means that we will pray earnestly for the lost, the discouraged or downcast, and our enemies. We are to "pray one for another," and with our prayers link all our efforts to help our brother. Dr. George A. Buttrick explains the place of intercessory prayer in this way: "So we are called to live in sympathy. Sympathy means not only 'feeling with' our neighbor's sorrow, but communicating to him our confidence that if we were in some besetment we could lift a banner above it. How, save by prayer?"—*Prayer,* page 112.

All around us is a world in need. Let us search out the heartbroken and suffering, speaking words of hope, doing acts of kindness, praying for their physical and spiritual welfare. By kind words and gentle deeds let us make the pathway easier for weary, lost souls. We are to reveal the spirit of heaven as it was lived by Jesus Christ. "Speak as He would speak, act as He would act. Constantly reveal the sweetness of His character. Reveal that wealth of love which underlies all His teachings and all His dealings with men."—*The Ministry of Healing,* page 159.

PREPARING FOR THE
FINAL CRISIS

ᴄ⌒ 12 ⌒ᴄ

An All-Out Conflict Is Ahead

WHEN the conquering generals of ancient Rome returned from the wars, it was the custom of the populace to celebrate the victory with a triumphal procession. The soldiers marched through the streets while crowds shouted *"Io triumphe!"* At the head of the parade were magistrates and senators; after them came trumpeters, followed by wagons loaded with trophies of battle. Next came captives, humbled by their chains. Finally, the hero of the day appeared in regal splendor to receive the applause of the citizens. Thus was a returning conqueror lauded in olden times.

Soldiers of our American wars have been welcomed home by friends and loved ones with celebrations and parades. The victors of battle have received tribute from the nation for their heroic deeds.

But far exceeding the glory of any earthly triumph will be the homecoming that awaits God's faithful warriors who have been victorious in the conflict between good and evil. With eternal glory heaven will honor the heroes of the cross "who have come out of the great tribulation; they have washed their robes and made them white in the blood of the Lamb." Revelation 7:14, R.S.V.

We are called to fight an "all-out war" against the forces that destroy the soul. The church of Christ must awaken now, for a halfhearted preparation will never give us adequate defense against the enemy. "The eye of God, looking down the ages, was fixed upon the crisis which His people are to meet, when earthly powers shall be arrayed against them."—*The Great Controversy,* page 634. God has warned that "the devil is come down unto you, having great wrath, because he knoweth that he hath but a short time." Revelation 12:12. We must answer these questions: "Am I ready to endure the final crisis? Am I prepared to meet my Captain when He comes?"

God will step in to shake the church to its foundation. We are told that "soon everything that can be shaken will be shaken, that those things that cannot be shaken may remain." —*Testimonies,* vol. 9, pp. 15, 16. Yet the trial will strengthen the faith of those who are true to God, for "when the storm of persecution really breaks upon us, the true sheep will hear the true Shepherd's voice. . . . The people of God will draw together and present to the enemy a united front."—*Testimonies,* vol. 6, p. 401.

Prophecies in the Old and New Testaments warn us that "the day of the Lord will come." It is when Michael stands up that the dramatic events of the last crisis begin to take place, "and there shall be a time of trouble, such as never was since there was a nation even to that same time." Daniel 12:1. The time of trouble is a part of the great controversy that has been going on since Adam and Eve succumbed to Satan's temptation. Those who have stood unflinchingly for right, who have refused to receive the mark of the beast or believe false doctrines will suffer the wrath of the enemy. "When Christ shall cease His work as Mediator in man's behalf, then this time of trouble will begin. Then the case of every soul will have been decided, and there will be no atoning blood to cleanse from sin."—*Patriarchs and Prophets,* page 201.

"Great and terrible" is "the day of the Lord's vengeance." Joel 2:31; Isaiah 34:8. It is a "dreadful day," for man must stand alone as fiery trials sweep about him. Malachi 4:5. At this time the judgments of God fall upon sinners in the form of the seven last plagues. The prophet Jeremiah compares the ordeal of the remnant church to the long night of Jacob's wrestling. "Alas! for that day is great, so that none is like it: it is even the time of Jacob's trouble; but he shall be saved out of it." Jeremiah 30:7.

"Jacob's experience during that night of wrestling and anguish represents the trial through which the people of God must pass just before Christ's second coming. . . . As Jacob was threatened with death by his angry brother, so the people of God will be in peril from the wicked who are seeking to destroy them. And as the patriarch wrestled all night for deliverance from the hand of Esau, so the righteous will cry to God day and night for deliverance from the enemies that surround them."—*Patriarchs and Prophets,* page 201.

The Door of Mercy Closes

When the last opportunity for salvation has been given, a solemn edict from heaven comes to a judgment-bound world. The proclamation declares that every individual's case is to remain unchanged as of that moment: "He that is unjust, let him be unjust still: and he which is filthy, let him be filthy still: and he that is righteous, let him be righteous still: and he that is holy, let him be holy still. And, behold, I come quickly." Revelation 22:11, 12.

Daniel Webster once said that the most momentous question every human being must face is: "What is my personal accountability to God?" In the final crisis every human being is responsible for his own record. Our Saviour will have finished His ministration in the heavenly sanctuary, and in the time of trouble each person must stand alone. "Those who are living upon the earth when the intercession of Christ shall cease in the sanctuary above, are to stand in the sight of a holy God without a mediator."—*The Great Controversy,* page 425.

The word of God will be a citadel of strength to the remnant people in the day of temptation. Like their Saviour they will face the doubts and denials with "It is written." But the multitudes who have spurned truth in the day of opportunity will not find it though they search frantically. "Behold, the days come, saith the Lord God, that I will send a famine in the land, not a famine of bread, nor a thirst for water, but of hearing the words of the Lord: and they shall wander from sea to sea, and from the north even to the east, they shall run to and fro to seek the word of the Lord, and shall not find it." Amos 8:11, 12.

In the Hour of Trial

The Scriptures must become for men and women today what it was for their forefathers in earlier generations—the safeguard of Christian living. The admonition is given: "Study your Bible as you have never studied it before. Unless you arise to a higher, holier state in your religious life, you will not be ready for the appearing of our Lord."—*Testimonies,* vol. 5, p. 717.

The worth of a soldier is revealed in the way he faces the enemy, not how proud he is on the parade ground. In like manner, God's warriors receive their baptism of fire in the final conflict against evil. In that day neither position, degrees, nor wealth will keep us from disaster; we must depend wholly upon the promises of Jesus, for He has said, "My grace is sufficient for thee." 2 Corinthians 12:9.

A complaining Christian once said to a friend, "I simply cannot stand all the trials and sorrows that come to me. I wish I had never been made."

The wise friend replied, "You aren't made, my dear. You are only in the process of being made by all the experiences of life. That is how you develop character."

We become impatient with God's plan for us, and we rebel against the refining process; but this is a necessary part in the creation of character that will endure the last conflict. How difficult it is for us to be patient. It is not easy to "quietly wait for the salvation of the Lord." Yet God has been waiting thousands of years for men to finish His work in a sin-wearied world. To those who stand patiently, claiming the Lord's promise of salvation, come these words: "Because you have kept My word of patient endurance, I will keep you from the hour of trial which is coming on the whole world, to try those who dwell upon the earth." Revelation 3:10, R.S.V.

"Patient endurance." How few know the meaning of the words, yet how important it will be in the days ahead. When a traveler prepares to go on a journey, he is not waiting for his train or plane until he has purchased his ticket, checked his baggage, and made all final arrangements for leaving. Then, and only then, is he *waiting* for his train. In like manner we are not waiting for our Lord's return until we have every preparation completed and we are dedicated to that one event.

Our courage can be strong in the furnace of affliction, and we can have peace if the faith of Jesus possesses us. Not long ago I saw a dog chasing pigeons in a city park. The birds never seemed to be agitated or worried, for as danger approached they simply flew out of reach. Knowing they had wings they could well afford to be calm. Do we have wings of faith so that we may "mount up with wings as eagles"? Can we run and not be weary? Can we walk in the darkness and not be afraid? Isaiah 40:31.

"Though God's people will be surrounded by enemies who are bent upon their destruction, yet the anguish which they suffer is not a dread of persecution for the truth's sake; they fear that every sin has not been repented of, and that through some fault in themselves they will fail to realize the fulfillment of the Saviour's promise, 'I will keep thee from the hour of temptation, which shall come upon all the world.'"—*The Great Controversy,* page 619.

When all human help vanishes and the enemies of truth are ready to surround and destroy God's people, the Eternal One will shelter them in His pavilion. Sweet will be the promise: "There shall no evil befall thee, neither shall any plague come nigh thy dwelling." Psalm 91:10. Though the crisis may be fearful, yet the rainbow of God's love will be seen by every trusting child of God.

Wrestling With God

As we approach the time of Jacob's trouble we may be assured that God will not forget His children. "He that walketh righteously, and speaketh uprightly . . . shall dwell on high: his place of defense shall be the munitions of rocks: bread shall be given him; his waters shall be sure." Isaiah 33:15, 16. Yes, we shall know hunger and weariness; but as Jacob prevailed in the midnight struggle, so we may persevere and triumph.

"The people of God will not be free from suffering; but while persecuted and distressed, while they endure privation, and suffer for want of food, they will not be left to perish. That God who cared for Elijah, will not pass by one of His self-sacrificing children. He who numbers the hairs of their head, will care for them; and in time of famine they shall be satisfied. While the wicked are dying from hunger and pestilence, angels will shield the righteous, and supply their wants."—*The Great Controversy,* page 629.

As the plagues fall upon the world, leaders in governments will turn against God's remnant people and determine to destroy them. "A decree went forth to slay the saints, which caused them to cry day and night for deliverance. This was the time of Jacob's trouble."—*Life Sketches,* page 117. Again we are told that "when the protection of human laws shall be withdrawn from those who honor the law of God, there will be, in different lands, a simultaneous movement for their destruction. As the time appointed in the decree draws near, the people will conspire to root out the hated sect. It will be determined to strike in one night a decisive blow, which shall utterly silence the voice of dissent and reproof."—*The Great Controversy,* page 635.

In this hour, after probation has closed, the faithful remnant cling to the divine promises. They say, as did Jacob, "I will not let Thee go, except Thou bless me." They cannot comprehend why they must suffer; but, like Job, their faith surmounts the trial, and they hold fast to God. The patriarch of old was able to wrestle victoriously because he had confessed and forsaken his sins. "So, in the time of trouble, if the people of God had unconfessed sins to appear before them while tortured with fear and anguish, they would be overwhelmed; despair would cut off their faith, and they could not have confidence to plead with God for deliverance. But while they have a deep sense of their unworthiness, they have no concealed wrongs to reveal. Their

sins have gone beforehand to judgment, and have been blotted out; and they cannot bring them to remembrance."—
Ibid., p. 620.

The Hour of Deliverance

The midnight hour arrives, and, lo, it is the hour when the Almighty manifests His power to deliver His saints! There are upheavals in nature and a mighty earthquake "such as was not since men were upon the earth." The law of God is dramatically set forth to the inhabitants of the earth that all may know the eternal Ten Words, including the seventh-day Sabbath. Then the voice of God is heard proclaiming the hour of Christ's coming. In humble triumph the redeemed exclaim, "Lo, this is our God; we have waited for Him, and He will save us: this is the Lord; we have waited for Him, we will be glad and rejoice in His salvation." Isaiah 25:9.

The second coming of Jesus is a world-shaking event that will be witnessed by all earth's inhabitants. "Every eye shall see Him," echoes in our ears, and we remember that Paul said that the event would be heralded with a shout and a peal from "the trumpet of God." This is the triumphant appearing of the King of kings; for He comes in His own glory, with the glory of His Father, and the glory of all the heavenly beings. Victory over sin and death is a reality, and the universe is at peace once more.

Our Saviour is no longer "a Man of Sorrows, and acquainted with grief." Now He comes as the triumphant King who has redeemed His people from the slavery of sin. John presents the vivid picture in these words: "I saw heaven opened, and behold a white horse; and He that sat upon him was called Faithful and True, and in righteousness He doth judge and make war. His eyes were as a flame of fire, and on His head were many

crowns; and He had a name written, that no man knew, but
He Himself. . . . And the armies which were in heaven followed Him upon white horses, clothed in fine linen, white and
clean. . . . And He hath on His vesture and on His thigh a
name written, *King of kings, and Lord of lords."* Revelation 19:11-16.

Those who have scoffed at the prophecies concerning our
Lord's return will see Him in all His glory. Those who have
mocked His claim to be the Son of God will be speechless in
the hour of triumph. The words of the Master will be fulfilled:
"Hereafter shall ye see the Son of man sitting on the right hand
of power, and coming in the clouds of heaven." Matthew 26:64.

In this decisive hour the wheat will be separated from the
chaff. Those who have accepted the sacrifice of Calvary, who
have loved their Master and obeyed His commandments, will
meet Him with joy. But human beings who have rejected
every offer of divine love, who have spurned the messages of
warning against sin, who have sought their own willful, law-
less course, will hide in caves and mountain fastnesses. They
will cry to the rocks and mountains: "Fall on us, and hide us
from the face of Him that sitteth on the throne, and from the
wrath of the Lamb: for the great day of His wrath is come;
and who shall be able to stand?" Revelation 6:16, 17.

The redeemed are transported to heaven, where they gather
upon the crystal sea before the throne of God. They have "gotten the victory" and now they become a mighty chorus to sing
the song of Moses and the Lamb. Of this group one of the
twenty-four elders has declared, "These are they which came
out of great tribulation, and have washed their robes, and made
them white in the blood of the Lamb." Revelation 7:14.

As the triumphant procession enters the city of God, Jesus
bestows upon each one the emblems of victory. "The glittering

ranks are drawn up, in the form of a hollow square, about their King, whose form rises in majesty high above saint and angel, whose countenance beams upon them full of benignant love. Throughout the unnumbered host of the redeemed, every glance is fixed upon Him, every eye beholds His glory whose 'visage was so marred more than any man, and His form more than the sons of men.' Upon the heads of the overcomers, Jesus with His own right hand places the crown of glory." Finally Jesus speaks, and a "voice, richer than any music that ever fell on mortal ear, is heard, saying, 'Your conflict is ended.' 'Come, ye blessed of My Father, inherit the kingdom prepared for you from the foundation of the world.' "—*The Great Controversy,* pages 645, 646.

As we think of the glories that await us, we long to be triumphant, and we ask: "How can I be sure of victory?" God's Guidebook tells us plainly we cannot conquer through our own efforts. God gives "us the victory through our Lord Jesus Christ." 1 Corinthians 15:57. The cross of Christ is the symbol of our salvation; His victory is ours.

Willing obedience is characteristic of the remnant people. They will obey the commandments of God and honor their Creator, who made the heavens and the earth. They will remember the Sabbath day to keep it holy. And in their mouth is found no guile, for they will walk daily with their Saviour.

The last generation of men will bear the burden of the weaknesses of their ancestors because of the long course of sin. Yet out of this age of chaos, God will bring a triumphant people. "Wrestling with God—how few know what it is! How few have ever had their souls drawn out after God with intensity of desire until every power is on the stretch. When waves of despair which no language can express sweep over the suppliant, how few cling with unyielding faith to the promises of God. Those who exercise but little faith now, are in the greatest danger of falling under the power of satanic delusions and the decree to compel the conscience. And even if they endure the test, they will be plunged into deeper distress and anguish in the time of trouble, because they have never made it a habit to trust in God. The lessons of faith which they have neglected, they will be forced to learn under a terrible pressure of discouragement."—*The Great Controversy,* pages 621, 622.

The hour of triumph is near. May we accept God's salvation through faith and be ready, standing loyally under the flag of our mighty Conqueror. He says, "Behold, I come quickly." With John we can respond, "Even so, come, Lord Jesus."

HOMESICK FOR HEAVEN

⁓13⁓

The End of Sorrow and Suffering

ONE four-letter word describes the dominant emotion of our generation—*fear*. We live in an age of crisis which the historian Arnold Toynbee calls "a time of troubles." Nothing fits the traditional pattern of living any more. War's end hasn't brought peace; more educational facilities have not produced better citizens; the H-bomb does not promise to scare civilization into being good any more than stories of hell-fire made everyone good in the days of the Puritans.

Science warns us that we are depleting many of our resources and that the world is waxing "old like a garment." By promise to free men from ancient beliefs, science led men away from the Bible and away from faith in God. Today we find civilization speeding down a dead-end street with the end in sight, as the nuclear scientists declare that it is possible to blow up the largest city with a single bomb. Thus we might well end all culture and destroy most of mankind. Truly our world is out of joint, and no man is wise enough to set it right.

Uncertainty and insecurity produce fear in men's hearts. Shortly before he died, H. G. Wells wrote, "A frightful queerness has come into life. Hitherto events have been held together by a certain logical consistency as the heavenly bodies have been held together by the golden cord of gravitation. Now it is as if the cord had vanished, and everything is driven anyhow, anywhere, at a steadily increasing velocity."—*The Mind at the End of Its Tether*, pages 4, 5.

Instead of faith directing action, many of us are trembling and weak-kneed. We are afraid of our children. Young married couples are afraid to have children because of the uncertain state of society and the responsibility demanded of them in raising a family. Children feel the fear that grips their elders. They do not understand what it is all about, but the future looks dark through their eyes. A teacher recently told what an eleven-year-old boy answered when asked what he planned to be when he grew up.

"I need not worry," said the boy, "as by that time there will be nowhere to grow up on."

Humanity dreams of beginning all over again. Instead of the blotted pages of history, the sordid stories of individual failures, we would like a new book with clean, white pages. Human nature grows weary of miserable disappointments and frustrations. Each new year is a symbol to millions of persons of the new beginning they long to make. They would give anything to forget the hideous past. God is ready for the human race to make a fresh start, for we have His plan stated plainly in these words: "Behold, I create new heavens and a new earth." Isaiah 65:17.

Through the ages men of God have been homesick for heaven. Implanted within each heart is the longing for freedom from fear and pain, and the coming of peace that only heaven can give. The apostle Peter had this desire, for he wrote, "We, according to His promise, look for new heavens and a new earth, wherein dwelleth righteousness." 2 Peter 3:13. And the heroes of the eleventh chapter of the book of Hebrews —sometimes called the Westminster Abbey of the Bible—were not satisfied with their world after they had caught a glimpse of the heavenly home. "But now they desire a better country, that is, an heavenly: wherefore God is not ashamed to be called their God: for He hath prepared for them a city." Hebrews 11:16.

By faith every follower of Christ can claim an inheritance in the new earth, for we are "heirs of salvation," "heirs of the kingdom," "heirs according to the hope of eternal life." We can claim "an inheritance incorruptible," beyond the insecurity of a world of sin. Peter declares that it is "reserved in heaven for you, who are kept by the power of God." 1 Peter 1:4, 5.

Although we dwell in the midst of sin and death, we can look beyond the shadows and tears to the "new heavens and a new earth" which is being prepared for those who love God. "Let our faith pierce through every cloud of darkness and behold Him who died for the sins of the world. He has opened the gates of paradise to all who receive and believe on Him. To them He gives power to become the sons and daughters of God. Let the afflictions which pain us so grievously become instructive lessons, teaching us to press forward toward the mark of the prize of our high calling in Christ. Let us be encouraged by the thought that the Lord is soon to come."— *Testimonies,* vol. 9, pp. 286, 287.

Heartaches and Tears Are Ended

Tomorrow need not be a dim mirage for humanity; God will make it a glorious reality. Look at the fortune that awaits us in God's new world. The capital city of Jerusalem will have walls of transparent jasper, streets of pure gold, and gates of pearl. In the heart of the city flows the river of life. John, the beloved apostle, saw the glorious capital and describes it in these words: "He showed me a pure river of water of life, clear as crystal, proceeding out of the throne of God and of the Lamb." Revelation 22:1 The tree of life is in the midst of the city, and every month it bears twelve kinds of fruit.

A fortune which cannot be reckoned in silver or gold awaits you and me in that better land, for there we shall have peace of mind and enjoy perfect happiness. Most wonderful of all, we learn that "the throne of God and of the Lamb shall be in it; and His servants shall serve Him: and they shall see His face." Verses 3, 4.

As M. L. Andreasen points out: "When Christ leaves to come to this earth, God Himself comes with Him. Wonder of wonders! God Himself shall be with us and be our God."— *The Faith of Jesus,* page 566. This earth will become the capital of the universe. The sin-cursed planet, so long darkened by the powers of evil, will become the focal point for the inhabitants of unnumbered worlds. Those who have triumphed over trial and tribulation will have the privilege of ministering to the Almighty and to Jesus, the Lamb. We shall see Him who redeemed us, and we shall reign with Him for ever and ever.

In our pain-wracked world, men would give every dollar they possess to stop the suffering and to prevent the death of their loved ones. In God's new earth eternal health will be the gift for all. "God shall wipe away all tears from their eyes; and there shall be no more death, neither sorrow, nor crying, neither shall there be any more pain: for the former things are passed away." Revelation 21:4.

Those who are afflicted with ailments so common today will then be physically strong. "Pain cannot exist in the atmosphere of heaven. There will be no more tears, no funeral trains, no badges of mourning."—*The Great Controversy,* page 676. The topic of conversation will no longer be the recent operation or the new method of treating our diseases. That will have passed away!

No disappointments, no heartaches, no suffering! "The voice of weeping shall be no more heard," and "the voice of crying" shall be turned to laughter. Isaiah 65:19. The long-cherished and unfulfilled dreams of this life will then be accomplished facts. Age will be meaningless, for in eternity we cannot mark time by years.

"And the city had no need of the sun, neither of the moon, to shine in it: for the glory of God did lighten it, and the Lamb is the light thereof." Revelation 21:23. Night will not exist in the world of tomorrow, since darkness and God's presence cannot dwell together. "In the city of God 'there shall be no night.' None will need or desire repose. There will be no weariness in doing the will of God and offering praise to His name. We shall ever feel the freshness of the morning, and shall ever be far from its close. . . . The light of the sun will be superseded by a radiance which is not painfully dazzling, yet which immeasurably surpasses the brightness of our noontide. The glory of God and the Lamb floods the Holy City with unfading light. The redeemed walk in the sunless glory of perpetual day."—*The Great Controversy,* page 676.

The Promise of Security

In an effort to find security, men buy every type of insurance: life, fire, theft, health, accident, disaster, and old age. The fear of facing a bleak, hopeless future haunts every home in our world; but in God's better world that fear will vanish. We shall build houses and enjoy them; we shall plant and cultivate as we desire and reap the harvest without damage or loss. We will be able to make plans and see them completed. Today we are afraid of crop failures. The homes we build and the businesses we start soon pass to other hands. But in Heaven's new order there will be certainty and stability. God's promise of permanency is set forth by Isaiah when he says of the redeemed, "They shall build houses, and inhabit them; and they shall plant vineyards, and eat the fruit of them. They shall not build, and another inhabit; they shall not plant, and another eat: for as the days of a tree are the days of My people, and Mine elect shall long enjoy the work of their hands." Isaiah 65:21, 22.

Millions of weary, homeless refugees have wandered from country to country since war's ending, seeking a permanent dwelling place. They are the flotsam and jetsam of the tides of modern global warfare. Orphans and helpless aged persons feel the agony of being displaced persons who will never again on earth know the meaning of "home." Such suffering will be unknown in God's new earth. He promises:

"My people will abide in a peaceful habitation,
in secure dwellings, and in quiet resting places."
Isaiah 32:18, R.S.V.

No more bloodshed or violence will break out in the home of the redeemed.

The three words, "I am sick," will never again be heard. Isaiah 33:24. No hospitals will be found in that wondrous city; no institutions for the blind, the deaf, the dumb, and the crippled will be needed. "Then the eyes of the blind shall be opened, and the ears of the deaf shall be unstopped. Then shall the lame man leap as an hart, and the tongue of the dumb sing: for in the wilderness shall waters break out, and streams in the desert." Isaiah 35:5, 6.

Emil Brunner well says, "We do not know what lies on the other side of death . . . we cannot imagine what life would look like which was not marked with the stamp of death. We can only express what we think in futile negations, which say nothing, save that we have become aware to some extent of the negations which death brings into our life. A negation of negations, that is the formula for ideas of eternal life. 'And God shall wipe away all tears from their eyes, and there shall be no more death, neither sorrow, nor crying, neither shall there be any more pain, for the former things are passed away.'

"Life without cessation, joy without sorrow, power without limitations, fellowship with God without disturbance, time without passing away, physical life without the flesh, sight without the pale cast of thought, without the paradoxes of faith, knowledge no longer 'as in a glass darkly' or in a riddle, but 'face to face, even as we are known'—all this might be expressed in one sentence: God will be there, and we shall be with Him. He will be our God, and we shall be His people."
—*The Mediator.*

Insured Against Sin

There is one insurance policy that is given to every citizen of the city of God. The underwriter is our heavenly Father, and the guarantee is sure. The wording of God's promise is simple and pointed: "He will make an utter end: affliction shall not rise up the second time." Nahum 1:9. No pain, no sorrow, no death, mean only one thing—no more sin. Certain restrictions are placed upon citizenship in the new earth to protect the redeemed from sin. Of the New Jerusalem we read, "And there shall in no wise enter into it anything that defileth, neither whatsoever worketh abomination, or maketh a lie: but they which are written in the Lamb's book of life." Revelation 21:27.

God's law will be forever honored, and all who enter the city will keep the commandments of God. Revelation 22:14. We are told that "the nations of the saved will know no other law than the law of heaven."—*Prophets and Kings,* page 732.

The wonder city will be open to all nations of the earth; but only those who are victors over sin, who have followed Jesus Christ, and have allowed Him to rule their lives, will have a right to this Utopia. As the redeemed obey their Saviour they will learn more and more of His will for them. Heaven will be a school in which we are ever learning. To the student will be opened the wonders of true science, not seen merely in laboratory experiments or test tubes; but in the firsthand glories of all creation.

There we shall learn the full story of the plan for man's salvation, the ministry of angels, and the mystery of godliness. In the divine school we shall learn why the great controversy between good and evil was permitted and how God's love was manifest in every page of human history.

"In the plan of redemption there are heights and depths that eternity itself can never exhaust, marvels into which the angels desire to look. The redeemed only, of all created beings, have in their own experience known the actual conflict with sin; they have wrought with Christ, and, as even the angels could not do, have entered into the fellowship of His sufferings." —*Education,* page 308.

One course of study will be of great interest in the school of heaven. There "all the perplexities of life's experience will then be made plain. Where to us have appeared only confusion and disappointment, broken purposes and thwarted plans, will be seen a grand, overruling, victorious purpose, a divine harmony."—*Ibid.,* p. 305. I want to take that course and learn God's reason for our trials and sorrows, don't you?

The conflict is forever ended, and we can give eternal thanks "to the Father, who has qualified us to share in the inheritance of the saints in light. He has delivered us from the dominion of darkness and transferred us to the kingdom of His beloved

Son." Colossians 1:12, 13, R.S.V. If this home is to be a reality to us, we must bend every effort now to reach it.

If faith grips your life and mine, then we will never give up the eternal interests of tomorrow for the small, fading baubles of today. Let faith grip our hearts and fear will vanish, for "perfect love casteth out fear."

The most precious gift to be bestowed upon the redeemed is eternal life. Jesus Christ will present this blood-bought gift to us. If we accept His forgiveness for our sins and claim His salvation, we shall hear His words: "Come, ye blessed of My Father, inherit the kingdom prepared for you from the foundation of the world." Matthew 25:34.

Jesus has a plan for your life and mine. He will give us power to be triumphant in suffering. He will deliver us from this chaotic, sin-cursed earth and bestow a fortune upon us—a home in a perfect world surrounded by peace and security where we shall see our Redeemer face to face!